Globalization and the North

Impacts of Trade Treaties On
Canada's Northern Governments

By Noel Schacter, Jim Beebe and Luigi Zanasi

Globalization and the North: Impacts of Trade Treaties On Canada's Northern Governments

By Noel Schacter, Jim Beebe and Luigi Zanasi

Cover design by Studio 2 studio2@rogers.com

Book layout by Nadene Rehnby www.handsonpublications.com

Canada Cataloguing in Publication

Schacter, Noel

Globalization and the North: Impacts of trade treaties on Canada's northern governments / by Noel Schacter, Jim Beebe and Luigi Zanasi.

Includes bibliographical references.

ISBN 0-88627-383-8

1. Northwest Territories—Economic conditions. 2. Yukon—Economic conditions. 3. Nunavut—Economic conditions. 4. Canada—Commercial treaties.

I. Beebe, Jim II. Zanasi, Luigi, 1956- III. Canadian Centre for Policy Alternatives IV. Title.

HC117.N5G56 2004   330.9719   C2004-905306-X

Printed in Canada

Canadian Centre for Policy Alternatives
Suite 410, 75 Albert Street
Ottawa, ON K1P 5E7
Tel 613-563-1341 Fax 613-233-1458
www.policyalternatives.ca
ccpa@policyalternatives.ca

Contents

PART ONE   Introduction 5

PART TWO   Summary 7

PART THREE   Background on the Northern Territories 14
                1. Governance 15
                2. Society 17
                3. Economy 20
                4. Environment 22

PART FOUR   Key Issues for the North 25
                1. Governance 26
                2. Society 28
                3. Economy 30
                4. Environment 33

PART FIVE   Background on Trade and Investment Treaties 35
                1. Trade Treaties and Organizations 36
                2. Trade Treaty Principles and Rules 38

PART SIX   Impact of Trade Treaties on Key Northern Issues 47
                1. Governance 47
                2. Health Care 52
                3. Economic Development 66
                4. Infrastructure 74
                5. Environment 79

PART SEVEN   Key Findings and Conclusions 103

Acronyms   110

PART ONE

Introduction

C anada's three northern territories are entering an era of major economic and political development. Economically, they are experiencing one of their periodic resource booms. There has been a revival of the proposals for a major gas pipeline from the Arctic Ocean to southern markets. This comes on top of the discovery (and now production) of diamonds, a very high-value product. Northern communities are looking forward not only to the direct economic benefits these projects can bring, but also to the economic diversification and social infrastructure they can help to finance.

Politically, the northern territories are in much better positions to build their economies with these developments. The territorial governments have won a wide range of provincial-like powers over the past three decades, including more control over the use of and benefits from natural resources. Aboriginal land claims have been recognized and largely settled over the same period, an important prerequisite for widespread resource development. First Nations now have viable voices in both their own areas and in the larger societies of which they are a part, some entrenched environmental protections, and the resources to participate in economic development. This tends to encourage them to participate in, rather than oppose, major resource developments, as they did in the past to gain recognition of their rights. Finally, the creation of the separate territory of Nunavut in the Eastern Arctic has resolved a long-standing division in the Northwest Territories.

Still, there are a large number of economic and political players in the North. The federal government retains significant control over resources and approval processes. The territorial governments must balance their needs for tax and resources revenues with their interests in maximizing local economic benefits. Aboriginal governments have achieved a new degree of local control over resources, but are reliant on outside investment to finance their roles in major developments. Large multinational corporations are seeking access to resources and local partners for joint ventures in resource development.

The North needs carefully designed policies to ensure that northern communities reap as much benefit as possible from new resource projects, that economic growth contributes to socially and environmentally sustainable growth in the North, and that territorial, Aboriginal and community governments are strengthened and made more responsive to northerners.

While the northern context has changed significantly in recent decades, so has the international context in which national and local governments operate. The new context includes both continental and global trade treaties that Canada has signed. The general theme of these treaties is to open local markets to foreign competition by limiting government's ability to regulate corporations and by privatizing public services. The restrictive rules apply to all levels of government (territorial, Aboriginal and municipal, as well as federal and provincial), all agencies of governments, and all activities of governments. The restrictions apply not just to the movement of goods, but also to investment and the provision of public and private services. The treaties are unbalanced and favour global corporate interests over local economic interests, as well as over non-commercial values and interests such as public health and the environment.

> There is a fundamental conflict between the need for northern governments to play an active role in economic development and the basic commercial objectives of a variety of trade agreements.

As northerners are aware, even more than other Canadians, a thinly populated and developed society needs public organizations to express, protect, and promote the needs of their citizens and communities. This paper looks in detail at what activities of northern organizations and communities will be affected and how they will be affected by the stringent new trade rules now in force. As will be seen, there is a fundamental conflict between the need for northern governments to play an active role in economic development and the basic commercial objectives of a variety of trade agreements.

PART 2

Summary

Background on Northern Territories

Though the North shares much with the rest of the country, the three territories are quite different from the southern provinces and even from each other. The introductory section of this report describes these geographic, environmental, social, economic, legal, and political differences.

The Yukon is a northern extension of the Coast and Rocky Mountains, drained by the Yukon River to the Pacific. Its salmon runs are similar to British Columbia's, and are the basis of the traditional Aboriginal economy, along with moose, caribou, and small game. The NWT is partly an extension of the Canadian Shield and partly coastal plains, divided by the Arctic tree line. The large caribou herds that are the basis of Aboriginal subsistence migrate across the territory. In contrast, Nunavut is mostly a maritime culture, from Hudson Bay to the Arctic archipelago, rich in marine mammals and fish, with caribou herds roaming the treeless tundra.

The Yukon is the most Europeanized territory, the result of waves of immigrants since the Klondike Gold Rush coming as soldiers, miners and public servants. Three-quarters of the 30,000 people live in the capital of Whitehorse, the rest in a dozen small towns and villages connected by a road system. There are 5,000 Aboriginal people, and most First Nations have settled their land claims over the past decade, resulting in money, lands, and self-government powers. The Yukon has had an elected assembly for a century and an elected cabinet for a quarter of a century, based on familiar political parties. The federal government has devolved most provincial-type powers to the local government, including most lands and natural resources in 2003. The territory's economy has seen booms and busts since the Klondike, mostly with the opening and closing of mines. Government is by far the largest sector, though tourism has grown significantly.

The NWT is equally balanced between Aboriginal people and settlers from the south. Almost half of the 40,000 residents live in the capital of Yellowknife, 4,000 in Inuvik on the Arctic coast and the rest in about 20 small towns and villages. Yellowknife and some towns have road links, but several do not. Many non-Aboriginal people originally came as public servants, as government here, too, is the largest sector, with some mining and sporadic oil-and-gas development in the Beaufort Basin. The Inuvialuit settled their land claims 20 years ago, and most inland Dene First Nations are on the verge of settlements. The NWT was run by Ottawa—in fact, from Ottawa—until recently. Power began to be transferred about 30 years ago to an elected assembly and cabinet, which operate by consensus, not parties. Only control of lands and resources remains in federal hands.

All three territories tend to have very young populations, with the Aboriginal population growing rapidly, and high unemployment rates similar to the Maritimes.

Nunavut is the homeland of the Inuit, who form 80 per cent of the population, and was carved out of the NWT as a separate territory as part of their 1993 land-claim settlement. The new government formally began in 1999, funded almost entirely by Ottawa. It comprises almost the entire economy in the absence of any significant industry to date. Indeed, 40 per cent of the adults do not work in the wage economy, and subsistence harvesting is still very important. Most of the 30,000 residents live in a dozen small, mostly coastal communities, with only 4,000 in the capital of Iqaluit on Baffin Island, all of them dependent on air and sea links.

Generally, all three territories tend to have very young populations, with the Aboriginal population growing rapidly, and high unemployment rates similar to the Maritimes. They have access to most of the social services familiar to all Canadians – public education, health care, social supports – though often at a very modest level.

Background on Trade Treaties

The new rules for "globalization" of business and economies have been created and implemented through trade and investment treaties. This process began modestly after World War II, with the General Agreement on Tariffs and Trade (GATT) in 1948, signed by 23 industrial nations including Canada, to restrict government measures on the import and export of goods. Canadians are most familiar with the Free Trade Agreement with the United States, which was later expanded to include Mexico in the North American Free Trade Agreement (NAFTA) in 1995. Negotiations have since been under way to expand NAFTA through the Free Trade Agreement of the Americas (FTAA) for the whole Western Hemisphere. The Government of Canada also set up the Agreement on Internal Trade (AIT) with provinces and territories, with rules mirroring those in the WTO and NAFTA. So far, it has only been a political agreement rather than a legally binding one.

The global context for NAFTA was the growth of the original GATT into the much broader and more powerful World Trade Organization (WTO). This has grown to 146 countries and administers completed trade treaties, organizes negotiations for new ones, and settles disputes among countries. The trading system the WTO manages is based on 15 interrelated and legally binding agreements. Their main points are:

- They apply only to governments; there are no restrictions on corporations.
- They apply to all levels of government: national, sub-national, Aboriginal, local.
- They apply to all parts of government: legislative, administrative, judicial.
- They apply to all activities of government: laws, regulations, policies, programs and procedures, including unwritten practices – all called "measures."
- They apply not just to goods, but also to:
    - Services – the General Agreement on Trade in Services (GATS);
    - Investments – the Trade Related Investment Measures (TRIMS); and
    - Intellectual Property – the Trade Related Aspects of Intellectual Property (TRIPS);
- They are enforced with a mandatory and binding dispute process.

Here are the major aspects of most trade treaties:

1. National treatment: This is the key rule usually associated with trade agreements. National treatment means that nations must provide treatment to foreign enterprises that is at least as favourable as the best treatment provided to similar domestic goods, services, service providers, investments and investors. If the national-treatment rule were applied to public services, then it could lead to unwanted privatization.

2. Sub-national governments: While national governments sign treaties, they apply to their entire nation state, including all the "sub-national" governments within the nation: provincial, state, territorial, Aboriginal, regional, and local.

3. Absolute prohibitions: These provisions apply regardless of whether a measure is discriminatory or not. NAFTA's expropriation and compensation rules can apply even when a government is acting for a public purpose, such as protecting the environment, and require compensation for affected investments. The GATS market-access rule ensures that private service providers have the right to gain access to public services.

> The new rules for "globalization" of business and economies have been created and implemented through trade and investment treaties.

4. Exceptions: Both the WTO and NAFTA allow very few exceptions to their trade rules. Exceptions are treated as violations of basic trade rules for opening up markets and can only be justified on very narrow and limited grounds. While human, animal and plant life or health and environmental conservation can be excepted, there have been only two such cases since 1948.

5. Dispute resolution: Both the WTO and NAFTA have rules and processes to resolve disputes between countries. NAFTA also has an additional process to allow private investors to challenge government laws and other measures at all levels. The largest single category of NAFTA investor claims to date are those dealing with environmental and public-health issues.

Impacts of Trade Treaties on the North

A. GOVERNANCE

Nunavut and some Aboriginal governments are coming into existence after the creation of NAFTA and the WTO back in 1995. As a result, these governments are less likely to be able to access any exceptions or limitations from rules in these agreements. This will also be the case for newly devolved powers acquired by the Yukon and NWT after January 1, 1995. This lack of the limited protections available increases the risk of a trade challenge to a variety of government initiatives, in particular economic initiatives, which are often inconsistent with trade rules. Also, Aboriginal self-government powers enshrined in the Constitution are not reflected in trade treaties. This means their actions are denied even the limited protections afforded to the Yukon and NWT.

B. HEALTH CARE

Per-capita health-care costs in the North are about twice as high as in the rest of Canada. Even so, there is less access to medical services, and the health status of northerners is lower. There is a strong need to maintain public control and ownership of health services, especially in the North where private services would lower access to health care for many citizens. Also, northern governments want to develop more telehealth services, since this could increase the availability of services in remote areas and reduce costs.

Health services are covered under both the WTO and NAFTA. There is a concern that Canada's public health insurance is covered by GATS rules, mainly the ones on national treatment and market access. This leaves open the door to a trade challenge by another WTO member country. NAFTA's investor-state dispute process can also be used to challenge Medicare and to force governments to pay compensation to corporations. Both trade agreements are potential threats to any expansion of health services covered under Medicare, such as home-care and prescription drugs, as recommended by the Romanow Commission.

Future negotiations to expand these agreements could increase the risks of a trade challenge to health care. Of particular concern to the North is the GATS negotiation of electronic-commerce rules. These rules have the potential to limit government control of telehealth policies to ensure universal access and necessary costs savings while maintaining high quality of care. This is because trade rules lead to commerce-friendly regulations and even privatization that run counter to needs in the North.

C. ECONOMIC DEVELOPMENT

Economic-development policies in the North are important in light of the already high dependence on government spending in the economy. Efforts to add more value to natural resources or negotiate local economic-benefit agreements and to provide preferential treatment for northern businesses and workers are important vehicles to expand the economic base. Yet these initiatives are potentially limited by rules in trade and investment treaties.

NAFTA's investment rules limit any requirements to use local labour, business, services or materials in a project, regardless of whether there is discrimination or not. The WTO limits export prohibitions, potentially making a requirement to process raw diamonds in the North a violation of its rules. The present round of negotiations to expand both NAFTA and the GATS could increase the restrictions on governments to pursue economic-development strategies, especially relating to government procurement of construction, goods, and services.

Both economic and social development in the North is supported by public infrastructure. In transportation, northerners are concerned about postal services, which are the main method of transporting food and supplies to many communities. This transport is provided at about one-third its commercial cost. The U.S. Corporation UPS is currently challenging Canada Post's services under NAFTA's dispute process, which could lead to the loss of services and increases in rates for the North.

D. ENVIRONMENT

The North faces two sources of environmental degradation: local development of natural resources and international impacts such as air- and water-borne pollution and global warming. Efforts to protect the environment are deemed to be inconsistent with the basic rules in trade agreements and are allowed only if they meet the requirements of narrowly interpreted exceptions. There have been no successful defences of environmental-protection measures challenged in trade agreements using the allowed exceptions. But there have been several cases where environmental measures were struck down by trade panels in both the WTO and

NAFTA and where governments were forced to withdraw these measures and pay compensation as well.

Multilateral environmental agreements (MEAs), such as the Kyoto Protocol, are the most effective ways to deal with international issues. There are fewer risks arising out of WTO and NAFTA challenges for MEAs than for domestic environmental measures. MEAs are particularly important for the North, where there is a greater concentration of industrial chemicals and a greater threat from global warming. MEAs are essential for ensuring the ongoing viability of traditional lifestyles that depend on subsistence harvesting.

Conclusion

Existing trade and investment treaties pose a serious threat to northern governments' ability to choose policies that are in the best interest of their citizens, including health care, economic development, and environmental protection measures. The federal government needs to reconsider some of the commitments it has made in these agreements, especially its commitment to cover health services under insurance services in its GATS schedule of specific commitments. Furthermore, the federal government needs to ensure that vital public-policy options in all areas are not further restricted by the present round of negotiations in the GATS, WTO at large, and the FTAA.

> Existing trade and investment treaties pose a serious threat to northern governments' ability to choose policies that are in the best interest of their citizens

PART THREE

Background on the Northern Territories

As part of Canada, the North shares a great deal with the rest of the country: a constitutional federation, a liberal democracy with individual rights and common responsibilities, a mixed economy of large and small enterprises operating with public facilities and regulation, a network of modern social services, a multiculturalism based on the free flow of people into and around the country, and a vast land with rich natural resources. Within that context, though, the three northern territories are noticeably distinct from the southern provinces and from each other. Compared to southern Canada, the North is composed of even vaster landscapes and seascapes, with environments both harsh and fragile, very sparse settlement, and early stages of political and economic development.

The three territories are also distinct from each other. By several standards, they run a spectrum from west to east. Geographically, the Yukon is mountainous and nearly landlocked except for a short Arctic shore. In contrast, Nunavut is mostly coast and tundra. In the middle, the Northwest Territories (minus Nunavut) is a combination of tundra, coast and mountains. The territories double in size from west to east: the Yukon is half as big as the NWT, which in turn is half the size of Nunavut. Yukon lands are the most temperate and productive, the NWT mostly less so, and Nunavut is more of a marine culture.

Historically, the North was settled from west to east. First came Aboriginal tribes migrating east from Asia and then south thousands of years ago. In the past century, southern Canadians have settled mostly in the

Yukon, less so in the NWT, and barely at all in Nunavut. The Yukon has the relatively densest population, Nunavut the least. The Yukon has the most Europeanized society, Nunavut the most traditional Aboriginal one. In both cases the NWT fits in the middle of the scale.

Based on geography and history, most communities in the Yukon are linked by roads, some are in the NWT and almost none in Nunavut. Economically, the Yukon has experienced significant resource booms and busts and some diversification, as has the NWT to a lesser and later extent. Nunavut has almost no industrial economy, but conversely still has a strong and valued subsistence economy of hunting, fishing and trapping, much more so than the NWT and the Yukon. Politically, the Yukon has had an elected legislature (on and off) for a century, the NWT for three decades, and Nunavut since 1999, when it was split from the larger NWT. Different as they are, each territory's lands, communities and traditions are cherished by the Canadians who live there.

1.   Governance

Governance in the North has largely been in response to the pressures of economic development and subsequent population increases. All three northern territories are now politically self-governing, with all-elected legislatures and cabinets. The Yukon became a separate political entity in 1898 during the Klondike Gold Rush. Elections to the legislature were first held in 1905, though the territory was run by appointed officials until 1979. (The capital moved in 1953 from Dawson City to Whitehorse, on the Alaska Highway.) Since then, elected cabinets have had an increasing number of provincial-type responsibilities, such as education, and the federal government is relinquishing its control over land and natural resources. It now has 17 MLAs, of whom seven are ministers. Almost all candidates run for political parties, which form traditional Canadian-style governments and oppositions.

Historically, the NWT has been the residual territory of northern and western Canada after new provinces were carved out. For most of this time, it was run directly from Ottawa by the federal government. An advisory council of federally appointed local residents was created in the postwar period, and Yellowknife became the capital. The first elections were held in 1975 and a cabinet of elected representatives was created by 1984. The federal government has been devolving provincial-type responsibilities to the NWT in a similar fashion to the Yukon, at a slightly slower pace. It now has 19 MLAs, of whom seven are ministers. Almost all candidates run as independents, and governments are formed and function on the basis of Aboriginal-style consensus.

The Inuit population of the Eastern Arctic have long sought a separate identity from the Northwest Territories. This was one of the conditions of their Aboriginal land-claim agreement, which was reached in 1993. As a result, the federal government created by legislation a separate territory called Nunavut, which came into existence in 1999, when 17 ridings elected members to the legislature. All ran as independents, and more than half of them (10) are ministers, in an effort by the new government to strongly reflect the Aboriginal traditions of consensus and decentralization, with only executive functions in the capital of Iqaluit and operating departments in other communities.

Despite the political progress of the past quarter-century, the territories still have no formal constitutional standing in Canadian confederation. They are only legislative creations of the federal government. Nonetheless, pressure from territorial governments over the past two decades has led the federal government to devolve provincial-types powers such as health, social services and resource management to the territorial governments. All three territories are strongly reliant on federal funding for their government revenues. Nunavut receives almost its entire budget from Ottawa, the Yukon and NWT between half and two-thirds, depending on the state of their resource revenues (the Yukon has had gold and industrial metals and some natural gas, NWT has had gold and other minerals, oil and gas, and now diamonds).

> Different as they are, each territory's lands, communities and traditions are cherished by the Canadians who live there.

Governance in each territory is more or less affected by the self-government provisions for First Nations under their respective Aboriginal land-claim agreements. Nunavut was created specifically as a result of the Inuit agreement, though they chose public rather than strictly Aboriginal government. Nonetheless, most MLAs are Inuit, reflecting their 80 per cent of the population. The Yukon's 20 per cent Aboriginal population are Indian, and their self-government provisions are negotiated for each First Nation under an umbrella agreement, mostly for their internal affairs and for co-management of lands and resources and of shared social services.

But most public government leadership is non-Aboriginal. Again, NWT's circumstances are in between: separate agreements with the Inuvialuit (Inuit) on the Arctic coast in 1984, which is more collective, and with the Dene (Indian) of the interior in 1993, which has provisions for different self-government arrangements for each First Nation.

An important factor in northern governance is that Aboriginal rights and treaties are recognized in the Constitution (Section 35). This means that provisions negotiated and agreements ratified with First Nations cannot be changed without their approval or by amending the Constitution. In contrast, the territories themselves as yet have no recognized status in the Constitution, although over the past decade they have been included in most federal/ provincial/territorial conferences. The provisions of Aboriginal treaties – for lands, land and resource uses, social services, etc. – will thus be significant factors in northern governance for the foreseeable future, especially where they form a majority or large plurality.

Each territory has one locally elected Member of Parliament and one federally appointed Senator. Municipalities are created by the territorial governments, much as they are in the provinces. Finally, the Inuit have a strong interest in other polar Aboriginal peoples (in Alaska, Greenland, Scandinavia and Russia), which has led to the creation of the Circumpolar Conference, and all northern territories play a role in the Arctic Council of polar nations in North America, Europe and Asia.

2.   Society

Although the three territories have similar population sizes (30,000 each in Nunavut and the Yukon, 40,000 in the NWT), their demographics strongly show their different histories. With Inuit making up more than 80 per cent of its population, Nunavut is Canada's most Aboriginal jurisdiction, especially outside the capital of Iqaluit. Although Europeans and southern Canadians have been exploring the Eastern Arctic for centuries, there have not been any economic attractions for them to settle there. Because the Inuit never came under the purview of the federal *Indian Act*, they have been more able to retain their culture and communities.

Nunavut is the one territory where most residents do not live in the capital (only 4,000), though most communities are smaller versions of its coastal setting. Inuktitut is an official language of the territory (along with English and French). Forty per cent of the workforce does not participate in the wage economy, instead relying on traditional subsistence harvesting.

At the opposite end of the scale, 80 per cent of the Yukon population is non-Aboriginal, and three-quarters of the people (23,000) live in the capital of Whitehorse, a relatively urban centre by northern standards, in a mountain setting. Settlers have come in several waves in a little over a century: fur traders, the Klondike Gold Rush, the Alaska Highway, government administration, mines, tourism. The result is a society more similar to southern Canada, and traditions and activities are not unlike those in Alberta and British Columbia: political parties, community clubs, social and hobby groups, indoor sports, outdoor recreation. Nonetheless, Yukon First Nations were among the first in Canada to negotiate a land-claim agreement, and are preserving their languages, culture and subsistence harvesting. For most people, though, wage employment is the norm, if less so in rural areas outside Whitehorse.

Northwest Territories again is a society half-way between the Aboriginal one in Nunavut and the European one in the Yukon. Half the population is Aboriginal (Dene, Metis and Inuvialuit), half are recent settlers from elsewhere. Almost half the people (17,000) live in the capital of Yellowknife, another 4,000 in the Arctic coastal town of Inuvik, and the rest in two dozen small communities. Yellowknife, located on Great Slave Lake in the spruce-forested Canadian Shield, would be familiar to Canadians living in the northern parts of the provinces, though Inuvik, on the frozen coastal tundra with above-ground heated utility pipes, would not.

The mix of Indian and Inuit cultures has resulted in 11 official languages: nine Aboriginal plus English and French. More people work in the wage economy than in Nunavut, fewer than in the Yukon; conversely, there is more reliance on subsistence harvesting than in the Yukon, less than in Nunavut. Outside settlement has come periodically, as in the Yukon, for example, for oil and gas exploration in the Beaufort Sea area and lately diamond mining, but has tended to be more isolated and temporary.

Demographically, the North tends to have a younger population than the rest of Canada. In Nunavut, nearly half the population (47 per cent) is under 19; it is 36 per cent in NWT and 30 per cent in the Yukon. These figures reflect not only general trends, but in particular the rapid growth of the Aboriginal population over the past two decades (up 15 per cent in the past decade alone), in contrast to a nearly stable growth rate of the non-Aboriginal population.

Demographics, in turn, tend to drive the demand for social services in the North. As a region of Canada, the North has received a relatively high level of social services such as health and education, given its small communities in remote locations. Health, education, justice, income and social-assistance services are generally available in almost all communities, though they are more basic than in southern Canada. There are modest hospitals for common needs in the capitals, other large towns have doctors, and all but the smallest communities have nurses. Still, patients have to be flown to large cities for more specialized treatments. (The three territorial governments delayed signing the recent national agreement to improve Medicare, which they feel does not do enough to improve services in the North.) Most small communities have elementary schools, though students must go to larger towns for high school. Small colleges are located in Whitehorse and Yellowknife, with distance-education programs, too, and one has just opened in Iqaluit. The territories have income-assistance programs similar to those in the provinces (along with federal family allowances, employment insurance, and pensions). Social workers and other social services are available, depending on location. Social services are somewhat complicated by the Aboriginal services offered by the federal

Although the three territories have similar population sizes (30,000 each in Nunavut and the Yukon, 40,000 in the NWT), their demographics strongly show their different histories.

Department of Indian and Northern Affairs, which are being transferred to First Nations governments where land-claim treaties have been concluded.

Finally, the northern territories are strongly shaped by their transportation services, which in turn are based on the environments in which they operate. The Yukon, with a smaller area and a longer development history, has a road network that connects all but one community. Although driving distance to Edmonton or Vancouver is more than 2,000km, local distances are only a few hundred kilometres. Whitehorse has a short road link to the Alaska coast, which facilitates bulk imports and exports. Yellowknife is linked by road to Edmonton, as are several other nearby towns, and Inuvik is connected by a long Arctic road to the Yukon and points south. The Mackenzie River valley is supplied by barges and by an ice road in winter. Nunavut communities have no road links and are supplied by water and air, which greatly increases the cost of goods and services for residents.

3.   Economy

The non-subsistence sectors of the northern territorial economies have depended mainly on exploration for and extraction of minerals and oil and gas and, more importantly, on federal government transfers.

Government spending is the most important economic sector in the three territories. This has been true for many years, at least as long as statistics have been kept. It is not only true for the three Canadian territories, but for Alaska as well, despite its oil wealth. In many ways, the north's largest export is Canadian sovereignty. Government spending on goods and services is a much greater proportion of GDP in the three territories than in Canada as a whole: in 2001, it was nearly 100 per cent of the wage economy in Nunavut, 60 per cent in the Yukon, and less than 40 per cent in the NWT, compared to a little over 20 per cent for Canada. The relatively low proportion in the NWT is a recent phenomenon and due almost exclusively to exploration and development expenses for diamond mines and oil and gas. Before 2000, the NWT's proportion of government spending also was above 50 per cent.

> In many ways, the north's largest export is Canadian sovereignty. Government spending on goods and services is a much greater proportion of GDP in the three territories than in Canada as a whole.

While government spending provides a relatively solid and steady base to the North's economy, mineral and fossil-fuel exploration and development create strong boom-and-bust cycles. The NWT is currently in a boom portion of the cycle, with the discovery and now the production of diamonds, as well as renewed interest in petroleum exploration in the Beaufort Sea area and increased oil production elsewhere. On the other hand, the Yukon and Nunavut are facing mine closures and are currently in economic downturns, with few short-term prospects for improvement.

Other primary industries are very small in the northern territories. Commercial trapping, which provided the main cash income generator to First Nation people in the past, has essentially collapsed, with the value of furs shipped now in the hundreds of thousands of dollars rather than in the millions. Forestry is very small in the NWT and the Yukon, and non-existent in the treeless Nunavut tundra. Commercial fisheries hold some hope for Nunavut, while the Yukon has a small but increasing agriculture industry.

Most other industries are dependent either on the government or the resource sector. Electrical energy production is mainly government controlled (with a small portion in private hands) and regulated through public utility boards. Manufacturing is very small, with shipments of $14.0 million in the Yukon, $35.8 in the NWT, and $14.0 in Nunavut.

Services are very important in the three northern economies, even more than in the south, especially health, education, and government services. Also, the Yukon has a fairly large tourism industry, valued at $164 million (15 per cent of GDP) in 2002.

Transportation and telecommunication services are critical to the North, given the large land areas and sparse populations. Transportation costs are one of the main reasons for the high cost of goods in the North. Air cargo is used much more extensively than in the South. For isolated communities, air (and water links in Nunavut and much of the NWT) is the only way that goods can be transported. The road network is limited to the Yukon and the southern NWT and Mackenzie Delta.

Personal incomes and wages are high; the NWT has the highest average personal disposable income in Canada, followed by the Yukon. Nunavut is in fifth place after Ontario and Alberta. The high average incomes result from the relatively high-wage jobs in the mineral and government sectors. The high cost of living offsets the high wages, however, so living standards are not appreciably higher than in the South.

Unemployment in the North is higher than the national average, resembling levels in the Atlantic provinces. In the 2001 census, Nunavut had a 17.4 per cent unemployment rate, the Yukon 11.6 per cent, and the NWT 9.5 per cent. The unemployment rate for Canada as a whole is 7.4 per cent.

Also, the relatively high wages and incomes in the North mask the dual nature of the economies. Like many Third-World countries, the Canadian territories have a high-wage export sector (mining and government) combined with a low-wage traditional (and, in the Yukon, tourism) sector. A large proportion of the population lives outside or on the fringes of the market economy, and depends on subsistence harvesting.

4. Environment

As mentioned in the introduction, the three northern territories vary a great deal in their geography and environment. The most notable difference is the tree line, which divides the treeless Arctic tundra from the sub-Arctic boreal forest. This does not run evenly across the North, but angles northwest along the Mackenzie River basin, which has a slightly milder environment. The result is a southeast-to-northwest diagonal from the lower edge of Hudson's Bay to the top of the Yukon. Nunavut lies entirely above the tree line, and its lands are mostly inland and coastal tundra, broken only by a mountain range on the east side of Baffin Island, site of Auyuittuq National Park. More than half of the territory is, in fact, an Arctic archipelago, surrounded most of the year by continuous ice cover. This makes much of the territory like a continuous land-mass, which can be travelled across much of the year. On shore, there is continuous permafrost throughout the territory, with a shallow surface layer thawing during the brief summers.

In this environment, the seas are more productive than the lands. Millions of seals and other marine mammals that thrive in Arctic waters have been the basis of the Inuit subsistence economy, providing a source of both food and clothing. On land, the large migratory caribou herds, numbering more than 750,000, have been the main resource of the subsistence economy. In the modern era, seal and fox furs were traded commercially, before the supply of foxes dwindled at the turn of the century and anti-fur protests stopped the sale of seal furs in recent years.

NWT shares some of the environmental features of Nunavut – part of the Arctic coastline and archipelago and part of the Arctic tundra – but it is more diverse. Much of its environment is shaped by the vast Mackenzie River drainage basin, whose slightly milder climate prevents permafrost and allows the sub-Arctic forest to extend north of the Arctic Circle. Like the northern parts of Ontario, Quebec and the Prairie provinces, these lands are based on Precambrian Shield rock, with thousands of lakes mixed with forests and muskeg.

The Mackenzie basin also creates a set of navigable waterways that have been used in both historic and modern times. In contrast to Nunavut, the Mackenzie forests have long sustained a land-based subsistence economy of hunting (mostly for caribou), trapping and fishing. As in the rest of Canada, the arrival of European explorers and settlers led to a large commercial trade in furs of the large and small mammals of the northern forests. The forests have also been a source of subsistence building materials, though not on a large commercial scale. As elsewhere on the shield, a variety of mineral deposits have been found, and small mines have been opened from time to time. The latest discovery, in the past decade, has been an unexpected source of diamonds.

The coastal environment is quite distinct from the rest of the NWT, more closely resembling western Nunavut. It is an area of flat permafrost lands and shallow, usually frozen seas, which are not as productive as those in the Eastern Arctic, though there is a history of hunting whales, walruses and seals in the area. A major resource feature of the NWT coast is the discovery of a major petroleum field just offshore in the Beaufort Sea over the past three decades.

The NWT-Yukon boundary follows the height of land along the Mackenzie Mountains that rise west of the river valley. This area contains Nahanni National Park, where the Nahanni River cuts through a deep canyon on its way to the Mackenzie. Yukon lands are largely a northwestern extension of the Rocky and Coast mountain ranges, cut by deep river valleys. Most of the Yukon, in fact, looks more like British Columbia than it does like the other northern territories. All except the far northern tip is below the tree line. Like NWT's Mackenzie River, the Yukon River drains most of the territory's mountain ranges through a series of tributaries. Also like the Mackenzie, the Yukon

In this environment, the seas are more productive than the lands. Millions of seals and other marine mammals that thrive in Arctic waters have been the basis of the Inuit subsistence economy, providing a source of both food and clothing.

River basin has created a natural set of waterways. Unlike the Arctic drainages of rivers in the other two territories, the Yukon River drains (through Alaska) to the Pacific Ocean. This has created a set of salmon spawning routes that have become as much a part of subsistence harvesting as hunting caribou and moose and trapping smaller mammals.

The Yukon has more of a history of resource development than the other two territories. Its modest role in the extension of the commercial fur trade preceded the storied Klondike Gold Rush just over a century ago. This "opened up the country" to further exploration, which led to other gold and silver mines, then ones for industrial metals such as copper and zinc. There are also modest developments of hydro and forestry in southern Yukon and petroleum in the north. The Yukon has only a small coastline on its north shore and is cut off from the Pacific by British Columbia and Alaska, though it has access through coastal passes. The Yukon's southwest border with B.C. and Alaska forms Kluane National Park, site of several of the continent's tallest mountains, rising to nearly 6,000 metres.

The federal government still retains control of most lands and resources in the North, though it is in various stages of devolving control to the territorial governments. This has largely taken place over the past two decades. The federal government had made the settlement of Aboriginal land claims a legal pre-condition of local control of lands, waters, wildlife, fisheries, forests, minerals, and oil and gas.

In the wake of these Aboriginal agreements, Ottawa has been negotiating the devolution of resources. The expressed interest of each territorial government varies considerably. The Yukon has long had a strong interest in acquiring lands for development, NWT has wanted control of petroleum development, and Nunavut's priorities include sustainable wildlife and habitat management. The result is a variety of resource-management regimes across the North, with different mixes of federal, territorial and Aboriginal control of lands, waters, and renewable and non-renewable resources.

> The federal government still retains control of most lands and resources in the North, though it is in various stages of devolving control to the territorial governments.

Finally, it is an irony that the northern environment is both harsh and fragile. Though it is among the coldest places on Earth, it displays significant biological productivity: the marine life in the Arctic Archipelago, the vast caribou herds that migrate across the tundra, the dense nesting areas of migratory birds during the long Arctic summer days, the forests and salmon runs in the western areas. The long and intense winters, however, are a severe restraint on the ability of ecological systems to recover. Damage to the tundra lasts for decades. Signs of early exploration last for centuries in the eastern "Arctic Desert." The northern environment is known to produce large numbers of a few species that have evolved in fragile balance. Northerners live closer to their environments than most other Canadians and place a high value on them.

PART FOUR

Key Issues for the North

The key issues facing the North fall into four interrelated categories: governance, social services, economy, and environment. The issue of governance is central, as it has a bearing on the definition of the other three issues. Each Northern government reflects the unique make-up of its respective population, mirrored in the economy and its relationship to, and impact upon, the natural environment.

The federal devolution of provincial-like powers to Northern governments is an ongoing process that increases the authority of governments to better reflect the interests and needs of its peoples. At the same time, Northern economies are dependent upon the federal government for much of their income. This income provides jobs, services, and infrastructure. Economic dependency, however, constitutes a source of tension with the federal government. While this tension is common to federal-provincial relations, it poses greater challenges for Northern governments, as their new powers are not fully reflected in the constitution (excepting First Nations).

The global push for less government involvement in the economy, along with fiscal conservatism, is at odds with the needs of Northerners. The North cannot survive or prosper without strong democratic governments. Global pressures to impose a primarily commercial model of governance is counter-productive for Canadians in general and for Northerners in particular.

1. Governance

The biggest issue facing the three northern territories in the very long run is their legal status in Confederation. They are, in fact, legal and financial dependents of the federal government. This leaves the territories vulnerable in significant national debates, as was seen in the Meech Lake Accord, which traded off northern and Aboriginal status for other issues, and again in the recent national health accord, which the territorial leaders rejected as not meeting northern needs, although they were able to get it improved.

The political autonomy the territories have developed over the past two decades, with locally elected rather than federally appointed leaders, does give them a voice in national affairs, and they can find allies on different issues from time to time. But they do not have a vote and will not until they are provinces, which may be several decades away. Even then they will be small provinces, usually following the lead of the larger ones.

In the meantime, the territories are supplementing their political powers with real, practical authority over an increasing range of provincial-type jurisdictions as these are devolved from the federal government, such as land and resources, health care and transportation *(see chart on next page)*. To the extent that the territories are responsible for planning and operations in these areas, they will have a more credible voice in what happens to them.

Aboriginal self-government is a much more significant part of governance in the North than it is in the provinces. This will continue to evolve as practical land-claim agreements are reached and implemented and, in particular, as the Government of Nunavut evolves. Aboriginal self-government will have two dimensions of governance: first, its ability to manage and protect the rights and affairs of First Nations and their members; and, second, its ability to interact successfully with other public agencies.

Notes to Table 1

[1] Land-claim agreements of Inuvialuit, Gwichin and Sahtu Dene/Metis in lower Mackenzie region (7,000 of 20,000 aboriginal people in NWT). Now negotiating complementary self-government agreements similar to Yukon and Nunavut. Other NWT First Nations still negotiating land-claim and self-government agreements. This will be a changing situation over the next several years.

[2] All functions started with 1999 creation of Nunavut territory.

[3] Resource use and revenues, environment and economic development are jointly subject of discussion by federal government with NWT Government and aboriginal governments and organizations.

Table 1: Provincial-Type Powers in Northern Territories

Authority	Yukon — Territory	Yukon — First Nations	NWT — Territory	NWT — First Nations[1]	Nunavut — Territory[2]	Nunavut — First Nations
1. Resources	[3]		[3]			
A. Lands	No (<1 %)	8.5 %	No (<1 %)	13 %	No (<1 %)	17.5 %
B. Land use	2003	For B to E, control	No	For B to E, control	Share w/ Feds	Share w/ Feds
C. Environment	2003	of treaty lands	Some	of treaty lands	Share w/ Feds	Share w/ Feds
D Game & fish	1900, 1989	& about half of	Yes	& about half of	Share w/ Feds	Share w/ Feds
E. Waters	2003	board seats	No	board seats	Share w/ Feds	Share w/ Feds
F. Minerals	2003	Treaty lands	No	Treaty lands	No	Some lands
G. Oil & gas	1998	Treaty lands	No	Treaty lands	No	Some lands
H. Forests	2003	Treaty lands	Yes	Not yet	NA	NA
I. Revenues	Yes	Treaty lands	No	Treaty lands & some royalties	Share w/ Feds	Share w/ Feds
2. Social				[1]		[1]
A. Education	1972	1993	Yes	Not yet	Yes	No
B. Welfare	1972	1993	Yes	Not yet	Shared	Shared
C. Soc. Services	1972	1993	Yes	Not yet	Shared	Shared
C. Health	1993-97	1993	Yes	Not yet	Yes	No
3. Other						
A. Municipal	Yes	1993	Yes	Not yet	Yes	No
B. Transport.	1972-92	No	Yes	No	Yes	No
C. Power	1987	No	Yes	No	Yes	No
D. Justice	1971	Partial	Yes	Not yet	Yes	Partial
E. Econ. Dev.	Yes	1993		1984,1992,1993	Yes	Yes
F. Taxation	Yes	1993		1984,1992,1993	Yes	Partial
Retained federal authorities	Own most lands & resources. Some environ. areas.		Own most lands & resources. Most environ. areas.		Own most lands & resources. Share all environ. areas.	

Managing their own affairs includes using the lands and money received in land-claim agreements for a balance of economic, social and environmental interests, including jobs and income, culturally sensitive social services, and subsistence harvesting. In addition to land-claim agreements, local management is part of a broader national Aboriginal movement away from what has long been viewed as paternalistic management by the federal government. This is bringing more responsibility for areas such as housing and business development. Much of Aboriginal self-government is more than the municipal responsibilities associated with local government.

On a broader scale, the exercise of Aboriginal rights in areas of mixed jurisdiction will require federal, territorial, and Aboriginal tolerance and discretion in balancing a variety of interests. This is most readily visible in land and resource management, from the desire for local land use to the impacts of very large industrial projects such as pipelines. First Nations have significant legal standing from the Constitution and several Supreme Court decisions. However, in a federation such as Canada, as much depends on the effectiveness of leaders as on their legal powers, especially in areas of shared jurisdiction such as the environment.

2. Society

With racial relations on a better footing with the settlement of many Aboriginal land claims, the chronic social issue for the foreseeable future in the North is the level of services that can be supplied to small, remote communities. The North has traditions of both strong communities among First Nations and rugged individualism among European settlers. This is overlaid with the national policy in recent decades of ensuring that all Canadians receive approximately equivalent health, education, income assistance, and other social services. This is the basis of equalization payments to the provincial governments and of federal formula funding for the territories, as well as national family allowances, pensions, and employment insurance.

The debate in each territory is what types and levels of services are possible and appropriate, both across the territory and for different sizes and types of communities. This is compounded by the desires of First Nations to manage their own social services in more culturally sensitive ways. But even with federal payments and potential large resource revenues, there will be limits and trade-offs. For example, it is hard for families in small communities to send family members elsewhere for education and medical care. But even with improving distance education and health care, this will still continue; some services will not be available even in Yellowknife, much less Old Crow or Pangnirtung. The issue could be framed as what services *will* be available at each level. These are functions of location, costs, staffing, transportation, etc., as well as rising expectations.

The North is also caught in an enormous national and international debate about the role of governments in even providing some services. Generally, governments in Canada, strongly influenced by the United States, have been rolling back the type and amount of social services they offer, in parallel with larger or smaller cuts in the taxes that funded them. Health care is the most prominent example in Canada, with the federal government ending its deficits in the mid- and late 1990s by slashing its transfers to the provinces and even leaving the territorial governments, with their relatively small revenues, to make up as much of the difference as they could. This was accompanied by Ottawa agreeing to give provinces and territories greater "flexibility" to decide how federal transfers are spent.

> The North has traditions of both strong communities among First Nations and rugged individualism among European settlers.

While health care spending was generally cut less than education and social services, measures to freeze or slow the increase in provincial and territorial spending on health has led to increased efforts to bring in more private funding and services. The North cannot be isolated from this debate and, indeed, may be the most affected by it. Not only is there little prospect of profits to attract private health care to the North, but also the territories are strongly dependent on a comprehensive public medical system in southern Canada to back up their own local services. These trends are less strong in other areas such as education and social services, but they are not absent. If the rest of Canada is reducing public social services, it may not have much appetite to provide more in the North, including transportation subsidies. Northerners would also be strongly affected by reductions to national income-support programs such as employment insurance and pensions.

Within this broader context, there are a number of social issues involved in the cultural aspirations and needs of First Nations in society:

- What education systems can allow young people to retain roots in their Aboriginal communities and traditions, while also helping them succeed in society?
- What will be an appropriate mix of wage income, subsistence harvesting, and public supports such as pensions?
- What medical and other programs can enable Aboriginal people to lead healthier lives, for example, in avoiding substance abuse?
- What types of social services need to be developed to support Aboriginal families and communities, for example, in child adoption and the justice system?

These are a significant part of the evolving social fabric across the North, and the novelty of Aboriginal land-claim settlements means there are few clear indications yet of what directions will be taken.

3. Economy

Economic issues in the North are mostly related either to natural-resource developments or the need for economic development and diversification. For most Northerners, it is obvious that governments need to play an active role in fostering economic development – including in the Yukon, which has a generally more free-market orientation.

The northern economies have always been at the mercy of large resource developments, and these have created wide swings in economic activity. Nevertheless, the territorial governments continue to actively pursue mining and oil-and-gas development, often through subsidies, tax breaks, and other types of incentives. In the Yukon, for example, exploration companies can receive rebates or subsidies for hiring local workers. As well, there are subsidies for mining exploration and road building, and subsidized power rates have been used as incentives to attract mines in the past. Large natural-resource-extraction projects continue to be perceived as the major form of economic development suitable for the North.

Northern governments actively try to maximize local benefits from these developments. First Nation governments, in particular, insist on negotiating impact-benefit agreements with mining and petroleum companies to ensure they have preferential access to employment, training, and business opportunities created by the exploration, development or extraction activities.

Northerners are conscious of their dependence on natural resources and on federal transfers, and the need for economic diversification is a constantly recurring theme. Policies have been put in place to leverage territorial governments' spending power to subsidize local manufacturing and contracting. Both the Yukon and NWT have business-incentive policies that subsidize local construction contractors and manufacturers who bid on government contracts. The NWT policy provides a percentage preference to reduce the bid price of "northern" firms, while the Yukon policy gives a rebate to local manufacturing firms or firms hiring local labour on government contracts. Nunavut has introduced a contracting policy that assesses bid adjustments for contractors, with different preferences given for local ownership, Inuit ownership, local employment, Inuit employment and training.

As well, governments have been active in assisting other new industries to become established. In the Yukon, tourism is already an important economic sector, and the NWT and Nunavut governments are attempting to increase the size of their industries. Building on tourism, the Yukon is trying to develop a film industry and is improving its subsidy package. The NWT government has an economic-development corporation that invests in or owns and operates a number of businesses. The Yukon government also has an economic development corporation, but it acts solely as a holding company for the public energy corporation. The Nunavut government has a range of programs to support new businesses, including subsidies provided by the Business Development Fund, grants for small businesses, support for tourism operators and operations of the Nunavut Development Corporation

> For most Northerners, it is obvious that governments need to play an active role in fostering economic development.

First Nation governments make extensive use of government-owned enterprises and joint ventures to create employment and other economic opportunities. A major source of capital for this is the funding from the various land-claim agreements, some of which goes into economic-development corporations owned by the First Nations. As well, most First Nation governments, along with the federal government's Indian and Northern Affairs Canada in some cases, have active preference policies for Aboriginal-owned businesses in their procurement activities.

Economic development has been hampered by the lack of transportation and communication infrastructure. The lack of road and rail transportation makes air and sea transport much more important. As well, remote communities depend on subsidized postal services for the delivery of many goods, including food. The federal government, through Indian and Northern Affairs Canada, subsidizes postal rates for food in isolated communities.

(Road transportation has not been entirely deregulated. To ensure that all Yukon communities have access to freight services, a "reverse onus" policy is in place for new common carriers into smaller communities. New carriers can operate in a given community only if existing carriers do not object.)

The North is served mainly by four regional airlines and several small air carriers based in the North. Air Canada flies only to Whitehorse. Whitehorse has direct air links to Alaska and Germany, and Iqaluit has regular flights to Greenland. The four regional airlines provide scheduled service from southern centres (Vancouver, Calgary, Edmonton, Winnipeg, Ottawa and Montreal) to the territorial capitals and from there to other northern communities. Three of the four regional carriers are partly or wholly owned by Aboriginal development corporations. There are also a very large number of small air service operations that provide charter and cargo service to isolated communities and airstrips.

Although there is some low-cost hydroelectric generation in the Yukon and in the NWT, electricity in most communities is generated on a small scale with diesel generators. There is some experimental wind generation in the Yukon and Nunavut, while natural-gas generation is used in Inuvik, NWT. In isolated communities, fuel for electricity generation must be flown in, so electricity costs are very high by Canadian standards. Cross-subsidisation of electrical power is the policy in the NWT (through government subsidies) and the Yukon (through equal rates in all communities), while the Nunavut government subsidizes the transportation of fuel for electricity generation.

Telephone services are offered across the North by NorthwesTel, a subsidiary of Bell Canada, and are federally regulated. Service in remote communities is expensive and is usually cross-subsidized from earnings in the larger communities, mainly the territorial capitals. In the past, NorthwesTel's long-distance earnings were used to subsidize the costly local service. There is no competition in long-distance provision, as southern providers have show little interest in the North's small market. NorthwesTel is cross-subsidized by southern carriers to ensure that it has sufficient revenue to offer local service in all communities and is able to offer long-distance rates comparable to southern Canada. Telephone service and high-speed Internet service have been expanded in the Yukon through government subsidies for new installations. In the other two territories, dial-up or broadband access is still not available in many communities.

4.   Environment

Large-scale, long-term environmental issues for northerners are sustaining the existing environment and its uses, accommodating development pressures, and dealing with larger environmental issues from outside the North.

Northerners have a number of reasons for wanting to preserve as much of their existing environment as possible. At root, Aboriginal people have a long and ongoing tradition of living off the land, totally in the past and at least partially now and into the future. At the most practical level, subsistence harvesting is a viable alternative or supplement to wage and other income, especially in the smallest communities. Recall that 40 per cent of the people in Nunavut do not participate in the wage economy, with a strong reliance on harvesting. Beyond immediate needs, most northerners have a healthy respect for the natural state of their environments, living closer to the land and having more chance to observe and understand the lands, waters, forests, wildlife and weather than urban dwellers in much of southern Canada. And beyond even respect for the environment, Aboriginal peoples' living on the land for thousands of years is the basis of their social, cultural and spiritual systems; it is their individual and collective identity, to an extent that is difficult for others to know and feel.

In that context, northerners face the prospect of several large industrial developments and many small ones, about which they have mixed feelings. Perhaps the best example of this was the resistance of the NWT Dene to a major pipeline down the Mackenzie Valley in the 1970s. They felt at the time that it would disrupt their traditional lifestyles and prejudice their land claims and that they were not yet well enough organized to either deal with the problems or gain the benefits from such development. Now, 30 years later, the Dene-led NWT Government is an advocate of such a pipeline through their territory.

Similarly, the Inuvialuit of the northwestern NWT have had mixed feelings about the development of a major oil-and-gas field in the Beaufort Sea. But they have come to grips with it through a combination of proper impact-assessment processes, trying to preserve their subsistence harvesting and gaining local economic benefits.

Again, the NWT Government has welcomed the recent and very valuable development of diamond mines in the central NWT, which have the revenue potential to make the territory much more self-sufficient, while having only localized environmental impacts (in contrast to oil-fields and pipelines).

Nunavut has not yet experienced any major projects, while the Yukon has generally welcomed development since the Klondike Gold Rush. An exception to the latter is the proposed development of a large oil-and-gas field across the border near Alaska's Prudhoe Bay that could seriously disrupt the 100,000-plus Porcupine caribou herd.

> Northerners are likely to be seeking allies, not least the federal government, but also perhaps circumpolar organizations, to protect their envitonmental interests in the coming decades.

Finally, the North is not isolated from international, even global environmental phenomena such as global warming, weakening of the ozone layer of the atmosphere, and the polar drift of air- and water-borne pollution. These are controversial issues worldwide and likely to be resolved without much direct input from northerners as would be justified by the disproportionately large impact on their lives. For this reason, northerners are likely to be seeking allies, not least the federal government, but also perhaps circumpolar organizations, to protect their interests in the coming decades.

PART FIVE

Background on Trade and Investment Treaties

Although "globalization" has some personal and social dimensions, such as travel, culture and communications, it is mostly about large-scale economics. In particular, it is about large-scale corporations gaining power at the expense of governments (half of the 100 largest economies in the world are now corporations).[1] Much of this has been facilitated through trade treaties.

The process began modestly after World War II, with the General Agreement on Tariffs and Trade (GATT) in 1948, signed by 23 industrial nations, including Canada. GATT- member countries agreed to limit the tariffs and quotas that they applied to imports of goods from other member countries. Trade treaties played a modest role during the post-World War II era that saw the growth of the modern liberal state. During the conservative 1980s and 1990s, though, corporations were able to persuade governments to begin to use trade treaties to limit and then reduce the powers of public authorities. Other elements of this agenda included:

- privatizing public utility and transportation systems;
- reducing regulations that hinder business, such as laws on competition, finance, labour and the environment, and "harmonizing" them to lower levels;
- reducing taxes, debt and spending on public programs such as health; and

- competing to attract business not only with fewer taxes and regulations, but also with cheap land, buildings, resources, and even direct cash.

These practices over the past 20 years are changing nations, societies, and cultures. They also raise questions about how governments can continue to act in the public interest to provide services and control harmful activities.

1. Trade Treaties and Organizations

The GATT was originally a fairly modest treaty to limit tariffs among two dozen industrial countries. This began to expand greatly in the 1980s with the negotiation of continental (called regional treaties) and global (called multilateral treaties) trade treaties that covered more and more activities of countries. As well as covering many more nations, modern trade treaties are enormously more ambitious in scope. By extending coverage to trade in services, investment policies, government procurement and intellectual property, as well as trade in goods, modern trade rules extend far beyond commercial policy to restrict government measures in health and social services, economic development, culture, and other areas of public policy.

Canadians are most familiar with the Free Trade Agreement with the United States, which was the main subject of the 1988 election. It was later expanded to include Mexico in the North American Free Trade Agreement (NAFTA) in 1995. Negotiations have since been under way to expand NAFTA through the Free Trade Agreement of the Americas (FTAA) to include all 34 countries (except Cuba) in North, South, and Central America. The Government of Canada also set up the Agreement on Internal Trade (AIT) with the provinces and territories in order to create greater consensus on issues under international trade negotiations. The AIT now incorporates all of the major principles and rules contained in international trade treaties. To date, it has only been a political agreement rather than a legally binding one, as provinces have jurisdiction over most commerce.

The global context for NAFTA was the growth of the original GATT into the much broader and more powerful World Trade Organization (WTO). The eight-year (1986-94) "Uruguay round" of negotiations led to the creation of the WTO in 1995 as a permanent organization with 500 staff in Geneva to administer completed trade treaties, organize negotiations for new ones, and settle disputes among countries.

The WTO membership has grown from the GATT's original 23 countries to 146 (as of April 2003) – most of the countries in the world. The trading system the WTO manages is based on 15 interrelated and legally binding agreements. In addition to a modern version of the GATT, covering trade in goods, these trade treaties include:

- Services — the General Agreement on Trade in Services (GATS);
- Investments – the Trade Related Investment Measures (TRIMS); and
- Intellectual Property – the Trade Related Aspects of Intellectual Property (TRIPS).

These treaties are mandatory – all WTO members must ratify them and participate in ongoing negotiations. The WTO also includes certain optional agreements (called 'Plurilateral' agreements), including the Agreement on Government Procurement, to which Canada is a signatory nation.

All WTO agreements are enforceable through a mandatory and binding dispute resolution process. An offending country is threatened with trade sanctions if it does not cease actions that are judged to be inconsistent with trade rules.

Canadians are most familiar with the Free Trade Agreement with the United States, later expanded to include Mexico in the North American Free Trade Agreement in 1995.

In principle, WTO agreements apply very broadly:

- to all levels of government: national, sub-national, Aboriginal, regional, local;
- to all aspects of government: legislative, administrative and judicial; and
- to all activities of government, including laws, regulations, policies, programs, procedures, including unwritten practices – all identified by the term "measures."

While most treaties include reservations and exceptions that in practice limit their coverage, the basic architecture of WTO agreements establishes a sweeping scope that potentially restricts important areas of public policy. The obligation to participate in ongoing negotiations to extend coverage of WTO trade rules establishes a dynamic meant to con-

tinually reduce and eventually eliminate all "non-conforming measures."
While progress in this ambitious trade agenda is uneven, it makes for enormous uncertainty regarding public initiatives that could come into conflict with existing or future trade rules.

The growth from the GATT to the WTO went from a few élite countries to virtually all countries, from goods to everything in the economy, from voluntary to mandatory – from what countries did at the border to almost everything they do inside their borders. The rules they establish restrict the powers of governments, but include no corresponding responsibilities or obligations for private corporations. As we shall see, this major global institution is designed to transfer powers from democratically elected governments to international trade and investment tribunals using commercial values and rules.

2. Trade Treaty Principles and Rules

For the North, Canada's most significant trade and investment agreements are NAFTA, particularly its investment, services, monopolies, government procurement and intellectual property chapters and the WTO agreements, particularly the GATS, TRIMS and TRIPS agreements.

As usual, the devil is in the details. Domestic policy-makers must be aware of all the key obligations and how they overlap, diverge and interact.

The basic rules of these agreements are similar, but their precise scope and application can vary significantly. Interpretation is not always straightforward; applying the rules to a specific set of policy facts can be difficult. As usual, the devil is in the details. Domestic policy-makers must be aware of all the key obligations and how they overlap, diverge and interact.

International trade lawyer Jon Johnson provides a useful guiding principle for sorting out the variable policy implications of the parallel NAFTA and WTO regimes: "The practical result for lawmakers is that laws must conform to the more stringent of the two sets of parallel but somewhat differing norms."[2] This brief summary employs Johnson's principle by focusing on the most stringent provisions affecting Yukon, Northwest Territories and Nunavut in the respective agreements.

A. SUB-NATIONAL GOVERNMENTS

While the federal government signs treaties, they apply to the entire nation state, including all the "sub-national" governments within the nation: provincial, state, regional and local. Even though sub-national governments were not allowed at the negotiating table, the national governments agreed that all sub-national actions would be covered. This is set out in both NAFTA and the WTO agreements:

NAFTA Article 105: Extent of Obligations:

> *The Parties shall ensure that all necessary measures are taken in order to give effect to the provisions of this Agreement, including their observance, except as otherwise provided in this Agreement*, by state and provincial governments (emphasis added).

NAFTA Article 201: Definitions of General Application:

> *2. For purposes of this Agreement, unless otherwise specified, a reference to a state or province includes local governments of that state of province.*

General Agreement on Tariffs and Trade (GATT) Article XXIV: Territorial Application – Frontier Traffic – Customs Unions and Free Trade Areas

> *12. Each contracting party shall take such reasonable measures as may be available to it to ensure observance of the provision of this Agreement by the regional and local governments and authorities within its territories.*

General Agreement on Trade in Services (GATS) Article I: Scope and Definition

> *1. For the purposes of this Agreement:*
>   *a.*   *"measures by Members" means measures taken by:*
>   *i.*   *central, regional or local governments and authorities; and*
>   *ii.* *non-governmental bodies in the exercise of powers delegated by central, regional or local governments or authorities.*

Various reservations and exceptions limit the extent to which these agreements currently apply to measures by sub-national governments. While these limitations may limit the practical significance of some rules for northern territories and Aboriginal governments, for now at least, the principle of complete coverage of sub-national governments is intended to be realized over time and is an important factor in considering the implications of trade treaties for sustainable economic, social, and cultural development in the North.

B. SCOPE AND SAFEGUARDS

NAFTA is a "top-down" agreement, covering all measures and sectors that governments have not explicitly excluded. Canada negotiated a reservation (or country-specific exception) that excludes Canadian health care and social services to the extent that it is "a social service for a public purpose" from certain, but not all, provisions of NAFTA's investment and services chapters. All non-conforming provincial and local government measures existing as of Jan 1, 1994 are also protected by a separate reservation. These latter measures are subject to standstill, that is, they can only be changed to make them more NAFTA-consistent.

Certain GATS provisions — the most important of which is most-favoured nation — are also top-down and apply generally. But, in contrast to NAFTA, the most forceful provisions of the GATS are "bottom-up," applying only to those sectors that governments specifically agree to cover. Canada has made specific GATS commitments in mining services, marine transport, tourism, and other services of significance to the North. Canada has not made specific commitments covering "health services" as classified by the GATS. It has, however, made commitments to cover important health-related areas including, most remarkably, health insurance.

The GATS excludes services provided in the "exercise of governmental authority," which are defined as services provided *neither* on a commercial *nor* a competitive basis. Numerous areas of government activity are unlikely to benefit from this exclusion. For instance, because Canadian health care is a mixed system with significant private financing and delivery of services, this exclusion cannot be relied upon to fully protect the Canadian health care system from GATS rules.

GATS rules, unlike NAFTA, apply to subsidies as well as other government measures. In this respect, GATS rules are more stringent, although specific GATS disciplines regarding subsidies have yet to be negotiated.

Both NAFTA and the GATS contain general exceptions, which allow governments to argue that otherwise inconsistent measures are necessary to achieve legitimate objectives, including protection of the environment and human health. These general exceptions, however, have been interpreted quite restrictively by trade dispute panels. NAFTA's investment chapter has no general exception.

C. EXPROPRIATION AND COMPENSATION:

NAFTA Article 1110 provides that governments can expropriate foreign-owned investments only for a public purpose *and* if they provide compensation. NAFTA's investment protection provisions can be invoked directly by investors through investor-state dispute settlement. Neither of Canada's reservations protecting health and social services protects against expropriation claims under Article 1110. The existing WTO agreements contain no comparable investment protection provisions.

Whether a particular measure is an expropriation, and the amount of compensation due to investors, are determined by a NAFTA arbitral panel. Investors have successfully argued that non-discriminatory regulations which significantly diminish the value of their investments are tantamount to expropriation.[3] Thus, in sharp contrast to Canadian law, NAFTA panels have accepted that non-discriminatory government regulation can be equivalent to expropriation. Unfortunately, this extreme interpretation opens the door to NAFTA claims that environmental protection measures that affect a private investment or an extension of publicly financed services that displace a commercial operation are tantamount to expropriation and that compensation must be paid to U.S. or Mexican investors who are adversely affected.

Canada has made specific GATS commitments in mining services, marine transport, tourism, and other services of significance to the North.

D. NON-DISCRIMINATION PROVISIONS

Non-discrimination is the core principle of international trade agreements. *National treatment* requires that governments give foreigners the best treatment given to like Canadian goods, investments, or services. *Most-favoured-nation (MFN) treatment* requires that governments extend the best treatment given to *any* foreign goods, investments, or services to *all* like foreign goods, investments, or services. Even measures that are formally non-discriminatory can be violations if, in fact, they adversely affect the equality of competitive opportunities of foreign investors.

The GATS MFN obligation applies fully to Canadian government measures, including those of sub-national governments. NAFTA MFN obligation applies fully to federal measures affecting investment, and to territorial and Aboriginal government measures affecting investment, except for those measures in effect on January 1, 1994. Canada's NAFTA reservations shield health and social policy measures from national treatment claims *to the extent that they are related to health as a social service for a public purpose*. For scheduled services (e.g., mining services, marine transport, tourism, health insurance), the GATS national treatment obligation is the most stringent because, unlike NAFTA's national treatment rules, it applies to subsidies.

Economic development, health care, and cultural policies in the Yukon, the NWT and Nunavut include a myriad of policies that favour, directly or indirectly, locally-based service providers. Policies that favour local, community-based companies disadvantage foreign service providers or investors. Policies that favour not-for-profit providers, even though formally non-discriminatory, might also be construed as *de facto* discriminatory if local providers were predominantly Canadian and foreign providers were predominantly commercial.

E. PERFORMANCE REQUIREMENTS:

Performance requirements are conditions on investment used by governments to hold investors accountable to commitments to create jobs, purchase locally, transfer technology, or to achieve other local economic development, environmental or social policy benefits. They are important instruments of local and regional economic development and are commonly incorporated into Impact Benefit Agreements (IBAs).

> Economic development, health care, and cultural policies in the Yukon, the NWT and Nunavut include a myriad of policies that favour, directly or indirectly, locally-based service providers.

NAFTA prohibits the federal government from placing performance requirements on either foreign or Canadian investors.[4] Territorial and local government performance requirement measures that existed on January 1, 1994 are exempted from NAFTA. The NAFTA prohibition on performance requirements does, however, apply to all subsequent territorial or local government measures that condition investment on meeting targets for employment, local purchasing and sourcing, technology transfer, and other benefits.

F. QUANTITATIVE RESTRICTIONS

In scheduled sectors, GATS Article XVI, Market Access, prohibits governments from placing restrictions on: the number of service suppliers or operations; the value of service transactions; the number of persons who may be employed in a sector; and the types of legal entities through which suppliers may supply a service. Article XVI precludes such policies even if they are non-discriminatory.[5]

Article XVI applies in scheduled sectors such as tourism, marine transport, and mining services. Environmental protection measures commonly involve restrictions on business operations in environmentally sensitive areas. If territorial policies restrict the number of tour guide operators, or cruise ships in Arctic waters, for example, they could come into conflict with Canada's GATS commitments. Economic development or other measures that limit eligibility for government subsidies or service contracts to non-profit providers in scheduled services could also run afoul of Canada's GATS commitments.

G. DOMESTIC REGULATION

Ongoing GATS negotiations under Article VI.4 aim to develop "necessary disciplines" to ensure that licensing and certification, technical standards, and certain other domestic regulation of services and service providers is, among other things, "not more burdensome than necessary to ensure the quality of the service." In scheduled sectors, GATS article VI.5 already provisionally applies restrictions pending the outcome of the negotiations under Article VI.4. GATS Article VI is explicitly intended to restrict non-discriminatory regulation.

This article has raised concerns that, in the event of a challenge, WTO panels will be positioned to second-guess domestic regulators regarding the optimal or most efficient way to regulate services. Health care and social services are complex and highly regulated. Given the non-commercial values that underlie regulation in these sectors, oversight by an international organization committed to expanding commercial opportunities for foreign providers could be particularly problematic. As previously noted, Canada has made no commitments covering health and social services. Canada has, however, covered related services, including private health insurance.

H. MONOPOLIES AND STATE ENTERPRISES

The GATS and NAFTA restrictions on monopolies and exclusive service suppliers are broadly similar. Both agreements prohibit monopolies from abusing their monopoly position to compete in sectors outside the monopoly. Under GATS, monopolies must be listed as country-specific exceptions in committed sectors or eliminated. Under both agreements, a government wishing to designate a new monopoly in a covered sector is required to provide compensation. Compensation under the NAFTA investor-state process is in the form of monetary damages, while under GATS a government must negotiate compensatory trade concessions or face retaliation.

These monopoly provisions raise concerns about whether an expansion of a public service that displaces private providers could trigger an obligation to provide compensation. For instance, extending compulsory public health insurance (Medicare) to cover a wider range of health services (e.g., home care, prescription drugs) might attract claims for compensation from foreign insurers under either or both of these agreements. NAFTA's monopoly rules apply only to federal monopolies.[6] The GATS applies to federal and provincial monopolies. As noted, Canada has listed health insurance under the GATS.

I. PROCUREMENT

NAFTA and the WTO Agreement on Government Procurement (AGP) are broadly similar. Both agreements set out detailed tendering procedures that must be followed in all government procurements over specified monetary thresholds. Both also prohibit local preferences, local sourcing and offsets (e.g., local content, technology transfer or local economic development requirements) for covered public purchases.

Neither the NAFTA procurement chapter nor AGP currently apply to procurement of health and social services. Moreover, neither NAFTA nor the AGP apply to provincial, territorial or local purchasing. Because of these exclusions, the current impact of these procurement rules on the territorial and Aboriginal governments is minimal. However, the Yukon and the NWT (but not Nunavut) are signatories to the Agreement on Internal Trade, which includes rules on procurement by local as well as federal, provincial, and territorial governments. While these rules are the most significant aspect of the AIT, they cannot yet be enforced as effectively as are NAFTA and WTO rules.

J. INTELLECTUAL PROPERTY RIGHTS

Both NAFTA Chapter 17 and the TRIPS provide extensive protection for intellectual property, including patents. The TRIPS requires a 20-year term of patent protection. Both agreements permit compulsory licensing regimes, but only under very strict conditions.

Drug prices are one of the key drivers of rising health care costs in Canada. The ability to limit drug costs, as well as reduce travel costs, is a major challenge for territorial and Aboriginal governments in managing their health care services. Some provincial insurance plans have taken steps to ensure greater use of cheaper generic drugs. But many observers have pointed to the extensive system of intellectual property protection under international agreements as a factor restricting the availability of cheaper generic drugs.

Notes

[1] "Top 200: The Rise of Global Corporate Power," by Sarah Anderson and John Cavanagh, http://www.globalpolicy.org/socecon/tncs/top200.htm. Also see *Fortune Magazine*, July 22, 2002.

[2] Jon Johnson, International Trade Law, (Concord, 1998), p. 171.

[3] In the words of the Metalclad panel, "expropriation under NAFTA includes not only open, deliberate and acknowledged takings of property ... but also covert or incidental interference with the use of property which has the effect of depriving the owner, in whole or in significant part, of the use or reasonably-to-be-expected economic benefit of property even if not necessarily to the obvious benefit of the host state." *Metalclad*, para. 103.

[4] While the GATS does not explicitly prohibit performance requirements, its national treatment principle implicitly prevents governments from applying local content, sourcing and other performance requirements to foreign service providers in covered sectors.

[5] NAFTA incudes a commitment (article 1207) to negotiate the reduction of quantitative restrictions on service providers by federal, provincial and territorial governments, but the GATS obligations are more stringent in this respect.

[6] NAFTA Article 1505.

PART 6

Impact of Trade Treaties on Key Northern Issues

There is a fundamental conflict between the activist role required of northern governments to meet the needs of their citizens and communities and the basic commercial objectives of rules of the World Trade Organization, the North America Free Trade Agreement, and Canada's Agreement on Internal Trade.

This section examines how trade treaties affect northern territories in four broad areas: governance, social programs and policies, economic programs and policies, and the environment.

1. Governance

A. GOVERNANCE AND EXCEPTIONS UNDER NAFTA AND GATS

Over the past decade, the federal government has transferred numerous powers to territorial governments. This process is continuing and territorial governments are increasingly resembling provinces, in practice if not in name. The province-like responsibilities of territories may, however, lack the same degree of protection secured by provinces in NAFTA and the WTO agreements.

Both NAFTA and the GATS include exceptions and exclusions that provide a limited measure of protection for Aboriginal government powers established by modern land claims agreements. The scope of this limited protection is uncertain, however.

i. NAFTA

NAFTA implementation negotiations allowed each sub-national government the opportunity to have all pre-existing measures automatically covered by Annex I reservations. All pre-existing measures were those in effect as of January 1, 1994. Annex 1 reservations provide limited protection against some NAFTA investment rules, but stop governments from changing those measures in the future if they are made more inconsistent with certain NAFTA rules concerning investment and trade in services.

Annex I reservations do not provide protection against the most powerful NAFTA investment rules – in particular Article 1110 on expropriation and compensation. However, Annex I reservations do allow for protection against Article 1106 on performance requirements. This is an important exception, since it does not restrict territorial and Aboriginal governments' right to require local economic benefits as a condition for access to investment opportunities, such as for natural resource extraction.

Annex II reservations provide a higher degree of protection for otherwise NAFTA-inconsistent measures because governments are free to change measures in the future even if they are made more trade-inconsistent. Although annex II reservations could only be entered by federal governments, they can cover the measures of all levels of government.

ii. GATS

The GATS also allowed Canada, on behalf of provincial and territorial governments, to place limitations on its commitments in specific service sectors. Where the Canadian government makes a commitment for a service sector, such as insurance, it can enter limitations that specify government measures or particular services to which the national treatment and market access commitments do not apply.

B. TERRITORIAL GOVERNMENTS

i. *Yukon and Northwest Territories*

The Yukon and Northwest Territories were able to participate in the implementation process for both NAFTA and the WTO. However, some of their powers were acquired after the 1994-1996 period, when measures were being protected. Land use (2003), waters (2003), minerals (2003), oil and gas (1998), forests (2003), and the environment (2003) are powers that have been devolved to the Yukon government since 1994 (GATS) and 1996 (NAFTA). Any measures taken by the Yukon government in these areas might not be protected by either NAFTA Annex I or Annex II reservations or by limitations provided in Canada's GATS Schedule of Specific Commitments.

Having assumed responsibility for new powers after the initial NAFTA and GATS negotiations, the Yukon and the NWT have no opportunity to decide the reservations and limitations they wish to apply to trade and investment rules in these areas. It is unlikely that any measures exercised in areas of recently transferred jurisdiction would benefit from the NAFTA Annex I reservation for sub-provincial measures, which applied only to those in effect as of January 1, 1994.

Where the federal government has entered NAFTA Annex II reservations for federal measures, these reservations may apply to territorial measures after transfer of responsibility. If applicable to territorial measures, such reservations are very helpful since changes to measures can be made in the future even if they are more NAFTA-inconsistent.

Horizontal GATS limitations are likely to apply to territorial measures in newly devolved areas of responsibility. These limitations apply in all sectors and to all government measures, and include important safeguards for tax policy and a limited safeguard for policies that favour Aboriginal organizations and persons (discussed below).

Most GATS limitations in specific service sectors are unlikely to apply to measures in areas of responsibility recently devolved to the Yukon or the NWT. These limitations are generally specific to a particular jurisdiction, and would therefore not apply to a measure maintained by another government. Only those limitations that are entered for "all provinces and territories" would apply in areas of devolved responsibility.

The Yukon and Northwest Territories were able to participate in the implementation process for both NAFTA and the WTO. However, some of their powers were acquired after the 1994-1996 period, when measures were being protected.

ii. Nunavut

Nunavut came into existence in 1999, several years after the implementation of both the WTO and NAFTA. As a result, Nunavut measures may not have access to a number of the exceptions available to the Yukon and Northwest Territories.

The federal government would need to negotiate Nunavut's right to gain access to NAFTA Annex I reservations. NAFTA Article 1106 on performance requirements (leveraging local economic benefits and spin-offs) is excluded from application to provincial and state measures in existence as of January 1, 1994. If Nunavut lacks this protection, then its efforts to leverage local economic benefits from, for example, large resource projects could be more exposed to NAFTA rules through an investor challenge. It is unlikely, however, that investors wanting access to resources would refuse to negotiate an agreement containing performance requirements.

Similarly, the federal government did not enter any Nunavut-specific limitations in Canada's GATS Schedule of Specific Commitments. As a result, Nunavut does not benefit from the same degree of protection as other provinces and territories were able to achieve by having the federal government enter limitations on their behalf.

> The federal government did not enter any Nunavut-specific limitations in Canada's GATS Schedule of Specific Commitments. As a result, Nunavut does not benefit from the same degree of protection as other provinces and territories.

It may be possible to argue that measures in place in the Northwest Territories that were transferred to Nunavut are renewals of existing measures and are still subject to NAFTA reservations and GATS limitations as specified by the NWT. This view has not been tested by either WTO or NAFTA adjudication, and there are no relevant precedents.

C. ABORIGINAL SELF-GOVERNMENT

Aboriginal self-government powers are enshrined in the Constitution, as are those of the provinces. This fact, however, is not fully reflected in existing trade treaties. Like Nunavut, Aboriginal governments were not included in the negotiations that led to the formation of the WTO or NAFTA.

i. NAFTA

NAFTA contains a special Annex II reservation that applies to "Aboriginal Affairs." As noted above, in sectors protected by Annex II reservations, governments can adopt new measures or maintain existing ones that would otherwise be inconsistent with certain NAFTA provisions. The wording of the reservation states:

Canada reserves the right to adopt or maintain any measure denying investors of another Party and their investments, or service providers of another Party, any rights or preferences provided to Aboriginal peoples.[1]

The language contained in the reservation establishes a broad range of protection for measures that apply to Aboriginal peoples. Since Annex II reservations apply to all levels of government, it is to be expected that there will be the same protection for measures by Aboriginal governments that confer any right or preferences to Aboriginal peoples. As previously noted, Annex II is limited in its application because it does not provide any protection from expropriation and mandatory compensation rules under Article 1110.

ii. GATS

The GATS contains limitations on the national-treatment rule as it relates to "commercial presence" – the right of a foreign investor to provide services in Canada to Canadians. The Canadian limitation to commercial presence includes favourable treatment provided to Aboriginal persons or organizations for financial incentives to establish or operate commercial or industrial undertakings.[2] This limitation protects only certain kinds of measures (e.g., financial incentives) concerning services investment, and is therefore a narrower safeguard than the NAFTA reservation that applies to a wider range of measures affecting trade in services as well as investment.

In summary, territorial and Aboriginal governments may lack the same limited protections afforded to other sub-national governments:

- Because Nunavut came into existence in 1999, it may not have the limited protections under NAFTA's investment rules or the GATS limitations of specific commitments that are provided to all sub-national governments in existence at the time of implementation (1994) of these agreements.
- Aboriginal governments that have come into existence after 1994 will not have the protections afforded to other Canadian sub-national governments under either NAFTA Annex I reservations for investment provisions or GATS limitations of specific commitments.
- The broader NAFTA Annex II reservation for aboriginal peoples (see Annex II-C-1) is expected to provide Aboriginal governments with a higher level of protection than under Annex I.

- Powers devolved to the Yukon in 1998-2003 may not have the limited protection afforded to powers that existed in 1994 under NAFTA investment rule and the GATS limitation of specific commitments, except for applicable NAFTA Annex II reservations (such as Annex II-C-9 for Social Services) and those GATS horizontal limitations that cover all levels of government.
- The NWT would face similar problems if and when it takes over powers devolved by the federal government.
- The lack of even limited protections from trade rules could increase the risk of potential successful challenges from foreign governments or investors to measures relating to economic issues, social programs, and environmental protection, among others.

2. Health Care

Per capita health costs are higher in the North than in the rest of Canada. A 1998 Health Canada study measured the economic cost of illness across Canada. In the Northwest Territories (including Nunavut), per capita health costs were $5,244 vs. an average of $2,724 for southern Canadian provinces. The Yukon's per capita costs were $3,262.[3]

The Romanow Commission noted that the health status of people living in rural communities, especially in the North, was poorer than for people living in urban areas.[4] Life expectancy at birth is lower, infant mortality rates are higher, total mortality rates are higher, and unintentional injury-related deaths are higher than in urban areas.[5]

The commission reported that it is not only difficult to access diagnostic services and more advanced treatments in rural communities, but it is also difficult to access primary health services. As a result, people in remote areas must travel outside of their communities to get these services, increasing their cost burden and often removing them from the support of family and friends.

Access to health providers is another problem.

In northern communities, the problems are stark. About 16,000 people live in the most northern part of Canada, at 65-69 degrees north latitude (northern parts of the Yukon, Northwest Territories and Nunavut). About two-thirds of them live more than 100 km from a physician. And no physicians normally live above 70 degrees north latitude to serve the 3,300 people living there...[6]

The Romanow Report explores a number of options for improving access to health care, including telehealth. Telehealth uses information technologies to link patients in remote communities with health providers who can diagnose, treat, and consult at a distance.

> Telehealth is particularly promising for northern Canada. The Honourable Edward Picco, Minister of Health and Social Services in Nunavut, noted that telehealth has the potential to be a lifesaver in Nunavut... Ensuring access to health case is a daunting challenge when some people live in communities more than 2000 km apart.[7]

The Yukon is also exploring telehealth applications.

> Telehealth applications have been used to facilitate increased mental-health services, professional and continuing education, and family-doctor visits. Most communities in the Yukon are a five- to six-hour drive away from Whitehorse, and many are in locations that are often inaccessible by road or plane, especially in bad weather. There are instances where Yukon residents must rely on out-of-territory hospitals for specialized services. The cost of a single flight can be more than $10,000.[8]

As a result, the Yukon government spends 6.5 per cent of its budget for health and social services on transportation. Clearly, telehealth delivery options could be a major benefit to northern residents, especially those in remote communities, and could make more services available at lower costs.

Per capita health costs are higher in the North than in the rest of Canada, and the health status of people living in rural communities, especially in the North, is poorer than for people living in urban areas.

Beyond technological changes that can enhance health services, there is a more fundamental debate on how to improve the health system. Those who advocate market reforms as a solution to problems, and the way of the future, argue that the private sector is more efficient and can deliver the same quality of services at a lower cost.

The Romanow Report explained why this for-profit approach is flawed. First, for-profit health services currently being offered in Canada tend to "cream off" services that are less complicated and less expensive to deliver on a volume basis, such as cataract and hernia surgery. The public system is left with providing the more complicated and expensive services. Also, if a for-profit cataract surgery results in complications, the patient ends up in the emergency ward of a public hospital. These costs are borne by the public sector and are not factored into the costing of for-profit operations. Are for-profit services as efficient as they look?

Second, the Romanow Report notes that the evidence from the U.S. shows that quality of care is superior in non-profit settings.

> *More recently, a comprehensive analysis of the various studies that compare not-for-profit and for-profit delivery of services concluded that for-profit hospitals had a significant increase in the risk of death and also tended to employ less highly skilled individuals than did non-profit facilities...*[9]

In some instances, privatization of health services is occurring as a result of underfunding by governments. Diagnostic services, such as medical resonance imaging (MRI), are now being offered in private clinics for patients with enough money to avoid long waiting lists. This violates a basic principle of the Medicare system, which ensures that access to health services is based on need, not money. The pressure to offer such services privately results from underfunding public services.

> Diagnostic services are now being offered in private clinics for patients with enough money to avoid long waiting lists. This violates a basic principle of the Medicare system.

Those who propose privatizing health care as a solution to long waiting lists are often the same people who support tax reductions. In the 2001/02 fiscal year, total federal and provincial tax cuts are estimated to be worth $40 billion. At the same time, both levels of government are now increasing health funding after a decade of reductions. If only 10 per cent of the tax reductions were redirected to increased health care funding, this would add $4 billion or more than 50 per cent to the spending increases in health care. This would go a long way towards reducing waiting lists for diagnostic and other crucial services.

The cutbacks in health spending in the 1990s had the predictable affect of decreasing the level and quality of services provided, and put major strains on the system. This undoubtedly was a key factor leading to the public debate on the future of our health system. Between 1970 and 1990, the public sector accounted for 75 per cent of all health spending. Between 1990 and 1997, the public share fell to less than 70 per cent. The trend is been reversed as a result of recent increases to health budgets, but the result was that more money was coming out of the pockets of patients, the sick and, more often, the elderly. Arguably, this violated the original intent of Medicare.

The United States has pursued a mixed system of public and private health services, as has Canada. The role of the public system is quite significant in the U.S. in spite of its image as primarily a profit-driven system. Surprisingly, the U.S. government's spending on health was 16.7 per cent of its total spending in 2000, compared to 15.5 per cent in Canada. In 2000, per capita spending on health (in U.S. dollars) was $2,058 in Canada and $4,499 in the U.S.[10]

Even spending twice as much per person, the U.S. does not provide universal access to health care for its citizens. It is estimated that about 15 per cent of the population – more than 40 million people – are not insured at all. For those with private health insurance, it is expensive and often does not provide complete coverage. It is estimated that almost one-third of Americans would face personal bankruptcy if they required hospitalization for a life-threatening disease. About half of all personal bankruptcies in the U.S. are related to health costs.

While governments in Canada account for more than 70 per cent of all health spending, individual Americans pay more than 55 per cent out of their own pockets. In 1970, Canada and the U.S. each spent about 7 per cent of gross domestic product (GDP) on health care. In 2000, total health costs in Canada were about 9 per cent of GDP, while the comparable U.S. figure had nearly doubled to 13 per cent. The main difference is that the U.S. health system is controlled by business interests.

Amid all of these statistics are important lessons to be learned. First, while adequate health resources are essential, more money alone is not the answer to all problems. For example, health costs are higher in the U.S system even though there is no universal access. Government regulation of the system is needed to ensure universal access.

Second, the quality of care is not simply a function of how much money is spent on health care. Public delivery of health services, especially primary services, has proven to be more effective in assuring quality care.

Third, cost containment and greater efficiency are more likely to be achieved through a single-payer system, as with public health insurance, than through multiple corporate providers. Consumer Reports Magazine noted that the administrative costs for private health insurance in the U.S. are 20 per cent, compared to only 9 per cent in Canada.

Fourth, Medicare gives Canadian businesses a competitive advantage over their counterparts in the U.S. because of lower costs, better cost containment, and better quality of care.

In summary:
- Health costs are significantly higher in the North than in the rest of Canada.
- The health status of people in the North is worse than in the rest of Canada.
- Access to most health services is more difficult and more costly in the North.
- New technologies such as telehealth are being considered as possible solutions to the health care challenges in the North.
- The Romanow Report concluded that a publicly-funded and controlled health system is more cost effective and delivers higher-quality health services than a privately funded and controlled system.
- Recommendations from the Romanow Report propose to strengthen Canada's Medicare system through a series of measures to increase public control, as well as by expanding the system to cover new health services, such as medically necessary home care services.

The Romanow Commission on the Future of Health Care in Canada is a symbol of democracy at its best. Public policy is being debated and shaped through an open process, based not only on opinions of Canadians, but upon an evidence- and science-based approach to the problems and their potential solutions.

Another debate that could affect the future of our health system is taking place in Geneva, as 146 of the world's nations, including Canada, are negotiating the expansion of the rules for international trade in services. In contrast to the openness of the Romanow Commission, the trade negotiations are taking place behind closed doors; much of the debate is confidential, to be shared among the negotiators, but not available to their citizens. Canada is telling other nations its detailed positions, but it is not sharing the same level of information with us. The final agreement, whenever it is reached, will not be debated in Parliament or voted on by Canadians. It will be a *fait accompli*.

Before the negotiations began, it was agreed by the parties, including Canada, that no public services would be taken off the table in advance of negotiations, *so health services are part of the negotiations*. Canada has declared that it will not consider any GATS commitments that impair its ability to establish or maintain health, social services and cultural policies. It has also declared that it will not seek any such commitments from other countries. This is an important policy position to which our federal negotiators should strictly adhere, but it does not prevent other countries from seeking and negotiating commitments in health-related sectors. Because any commitments secured by one country is automatically extended to all WTO members, these commitments would provide market access to Canadian exporters of health services.

Some of the existing rules already affect health care, but the purpose of the negotiations is to increase the number of services covered by the GATS rules, as well as to increase the number and strength of the rules that will apply. Some of the new rules being proposed potentially could affect the future direction of Medicare in Canada. While the debate about the future of our health care system took place in Canada, the decisions may well be made in Geneva.

The North's greater health-care needs and higher costs both require a strong public system. New delivery technologies, such as telehealth, promise to improve health services and health outcomes while controlling costs. It is critical that these new technologies be applied according to the principles of our public Medicare system, such as universality. How will the GATS affect Medicare and its future?

Before the negotiations began, it was agreed by the parties, including Canada, that no public services would be taken off the table in advance of negotiations, so health services are part of the negotiations.

A. GATS

i. General Rules

General GATS rules apply to all services unless they are excluded. The two exceptions noted in the GATS (see Section 3.C.iv) are very unlikely to protect public health care. To protect health services based on the exclusion for governmental authority requires meeting a two-fold test: there can be no competition (a monopoly is required), and the service cannot be commercial in nature.[11]

Many health services are provided by both public and private sectors, and by both for-profit and not-for-profit providers within the private sector. The Romanow Report noted the increasing involvement of business in health services, as well as the expansion of user fees to offset decreasing taxes. Both trends would weaken efforts by Canada to protect Medicare measures from GATS rules under the governmental-authority exclusion. A background note from the WTO partially explains why this is the case.

The hospital sector in many countries, however, is made up of govern-ment- and privately-owned entities, which both operate on a commercial basis, charging the patient or his insurance for the treatment provided. Supplementary subsidies may be granted for social, regional or similar policy purposes. It seems unrealistic in such cases to argue for con-tinued application of Article I:3 and/or maintain that no competi-tive relationship exists between the two groups of suppliers or serv-ices (emphasis added).[12]

Some health services, such as long-term care, are delivered by both private and public providers. If patients pay a fee for a service, such as cataract surgery or a diagnostic service (such as an MRI), will the services be considered "commercial" in nature? Doctors now deliver most services for fees, albeit paid through the government. They operate as small busi-nesses using their own private offices, and some operate out of their own clinics. Would this payment system render all fee-for-service delivery as being commercial? We cannot defini-tively answer this question because there is no definition of "commercial" in the GATS.

A large number of health services may not meet the criteria for meeting the governmental-authority exclusion and would, therefore, be subject to the general rules of GATS.

A large number of health services may not meet the criteria for meeting the gov-ernmental-authority exclusion and would, therefore, be subject to the gen-eral rules of GATS. The final decision about which health services are covered and which is excluded from GATS rules will be decided by a WTO trade panel – not by Parliament or the legisla-tures of territories and provinces or by First Nations.

The general rules already apply to parts of our health system. For serv-ices that are covered, the obligations create restrictions on government actions. For example, if a territorial government allowed a U.S. business to deliver a health service, such as long-term care, businesses from other countries could not be denied reasonable access to providing the same service. The application of this non-discrimination rule could result in an unintended expansion of private health-care markets.[13]

ii. Specific Rules

Specific GATS rules are the most restrictive and require that member countries list services they wish to provide in a special schedule. In their schedule, countries can also limit the application of specific rules.

Canada did not list any health services in its schedule as of 1995. However, Canada did appear to make a major error in its GATS commitments.

Astonishingly, Canada covered health insurance in its schedule of specific commitments in the Financial Services Sector. Moreover, negotiators "bound" Canada's commitments in the insurance sector, meaning all future government measures affecting health insurance services must be GATS-consistent. Nothing in Canada's schedule excludes public health insurance plans from its commitments in this sector.[14]

This commitment exposes one of the main pillars of the Medicare system to potential trade challenges under GATS specific rules.

The market-access rule prohibits limitations on the numbers of services or service suppliers for a covered service. It also restricts limitations on forms of ownership of services and service suppliers, meaning that private, for-profit health-insurance providers cannot be excluded. The application of market-access rules leads directly to privatization. As Sanger noted above, the listing of health-insurance services are "bound." This could affect one of the recommendations made in the Romanow final report:

> *Recommendation 5:*
>
> *The Canada Health Act should be modernized and strengthened by:*
> - *Expanding insured health services beyond hospital and physician services to immediately include targeted home care services followed by prescription drugs in the longer term;[15]*

Because the commitment for health insurance is "bound," a country cannot make changes to restrict the level of market access that foreign commercial health insurers currently enjoy. The *Canada Health Act* prevents commercial insurers from covering publicly-insured health services. Extending Medicare to cover home care, or other services, would thereby reduce the market access of commercial insurers. This could provide a basis for a trade challenge under the GATS market access and monopolies provisions.

If, in the future, research and experience demonstrate that the public delivery of food, laundry or custodial services is superior to private delivery of these services, GATS rules can be used to block efforts by governments to deliver such services directly and exclude the private sector. The GATS, like other trade and investment rules, is a one-way street, allowing governments to change measures in scheduled services only in the direction of increased privatization and pro-commercial regulation. Once governments go down the privatization path, the GATS and other trade agreements make it very difficult to reverse direction.

iii. Negotiations for New Rules and Services

Negotiations to increase the number of services covered and to increase the number and strength of the rules have been under way since 2000. Canada has said it will not expand its commitments for health services, that is, make more of them open to private business.

But there are several other ways that new negotiations could capture health services. One of the most important sets of negotiations potentially affecting health services involves "domestic regulations." The domestic-regulation rule is found within the general rules and covers all services unless excluded. Domestic regulations include "… measures relating to qualification requirements, procedures, technical standards and licensing requirements… "[16]

For example, in the licensing provisions for hospitals and other health facilities, could government exclude business providers if the licensing requirements cannot "… constitute unnecessary barriers to trade?"[17] Also, licensing procedures for services cannot in themselves be a restriction on the supply of a service.[18] Could this mean that licensing procedures that restrict private hospitals could violate GATS rules? It will be important to monitor the outcome of domestic regulation negotiations to determine potential health-care impacts.

WTO negotiations are also under way on procurement rules for services. Procurement of services refers to the purchase by governments and other state entities of services for their use. The existing WTO Agreement on Government Procurement does not apply to provincial, territorial and local governments. Nor does it apply to any government procurements of health and social services. Negotiations could lead to procurement rules with broader coverage, either incorporated into the GATS or as a separate agreement. If procurement rules were extended to territorial government procurement of health services, it could prevent governments from requiring that contracted services be provided by non-profit providers. For example, some governments contract out long-term care services in a variety of areas such as homes for the elderly or the mentally challenged. Often, governments will restrict contracts for such services to local non-profit organizations because of their experience in, and attachment to, the community. Procurement rules would require open tendering to all foreign providers of long-term care services, potentially removing locally provided services.

Canada's own Agreement on Internal Trade (AIT) also comes into play here. At present, health services are excluded from the AIT. If territories, provinces and the federal government expand coverage to include health services, then how might AIT procurement rules interact with WTO procurement rules? Would the national-treatment rule then be applied as the best-in-country treatment vs. merely the best among sub-national governments?

Negotiations on electronic commerce are trying to develop rules to restrict government measures in this area. Electronic commerce is extremely broad and potentially includes telehealth and telemedicine services. Obviously, these negotiations are of critical importance to our health care system in general, but to the North in particular, given its unique problems and the hope that telehealth and telemedicine can improve access to health services while reducing costs.

The list of electronic health applications is very broad and includes:

- All forms of medicine at a distance – teleconsultations, telepathology and teleradiology, among others;
- Patient clinical records, data bases and information systems accessible by network;
- Public-health and community-health information networks;
- Tele-education for health professionals and patients, network research databases and Internet services; and
- Telemonitoring, telecare networks, telephone triage, remote home care and emergency networks.[19]

> Often, governments restrict contracts for long-term care services to local organizations because of their experience in, and attachment to, the community. Procurement rules would require open tendering to all foreign providers of these services.

There is an expectation that future worldwide growth in telehealth and telemedicine will be large. The projections for 2000 were that telemedicine and telehealth services revenues would represent about US$1.9 billion. Another US$3.9 billion was projected to be spent on continuing professional education, while online health information represents US$21 billion, or about 10 per cent of total Internet content.[20]

Telehealth and telemedicine are the new frontier of medical services. Unique challenges arise when a medical service provider lives in one country and the recipient of the service can be in another. Governments have yet to regulate these sectors in any meaningful way. This new technology raises a number of unique challenges for governments, such as the following:

- If a doctor in Houston, Texas, is providing a diagnostic service to a patient in Nunavut, then who pays for the procedure?
- If the number of service providers, in this case medical practitioners, cannot be controlled, then how can health costs be contained?
- How can the Nunavut patient ascertain if the medical practitioner on the other end is properly qualified?
- How can malpractice suits be applied across different legal systems?
- How can the Nunavut patient be assured that her/his personal medical information will remain confidential?
- What if the for-profit service being provided in Houston falls under the *Canada Health Act* and is covered by Nunavut's health insurance?
- How can Nunavut control the use of for-profit services to ensure that Medicare is not undermined?

No doubt these issues could be solved through a coordinated effort by all territories and provinces to establish control of electronically delivered medical services within the country. In addition, the control of electronic medical services across national borders could be regulated through a special international agreement.

But negotiations for cross-border medical service delivery are taking place through the GATS. The GATS is designed to liberalize services, resulting in privatization as well as commercially oriented regulations. This runs counter to the intent of a publicly-run and controlled health system, which is to ensure universal access, high quality of services, and controlled costs.

It remains unclear what rules will be developed for electronic commerce and how they will be applied under the GATS. If new electronic-commerce rules apply to all services unless those services are excluded, then health services can be put in jeopardy. Existing GATS exceptions and exclusions are inadequate to cover most health services, and it is likely those used for electronic commerce will be similar.

WTO negotiators have also agreed to a moratorium on new regulation and new taxation of electronic commerce, pending the conclusion of negotiations on new ecommerce rules. This suggests that governments will have to justify new taxes and regulations according to GATS rules – meaning that regulations and taxes will have to be the least-restrictive on private commerce as well as the least burdensome possible to achieve their objectives. Medicare principles will be secondary to the commercial principles within the GATS.

Telehealth and telemedicine are promising new methods of delivering health services. They can be used to strengthen Medicare by increasing access to essential services for northerners, by improving the quality of care provided, by allowing people to remain in their communities where they have more support, and by reducing the costs of care to governments. The application of GATS rules could undermine all of these objectives through new electronic-commerce rules.

In summary:
- GATS general rules already cover health services that are not excluded by the "governmental authority" provision or by the "exception" for human health, and could be used to increase unwanted privatization.
- Exceptions for health and governmental authority are weak and unlikely to protect Medicare from GATS challenges using either general or specific rules.
- Specific rules under the GATS includes national-treatment and market-access provisions, both of which can lead to privatization of health services.
- Market-access rules undermine cost-control measures by governments, since they do not allow for restrictions on the number of service providers.
- The GATS national treatment and market access rules apply to Canadian government measures affecting health insurance, which is included in Canada's specific commitments.
- Canada's health-insurance commitment is "bound," meaning that the addition of home-care or other services to Medicare coverage in the future could violate GATS rules.
- Negotiations to expand the number of public services covered by trade rules and to increase the number and strength of GATS rules are well under way.

- Domestic regulations dealing with issues such as licensing of facilities and qualifications of professionals are being negotiated and will apply to all services, including health services, unless excluded.
- Domestic regulations could lead to privatizing health services, as well as to limiting standards and qualifications in order to ensure access to health services markets by foreign, for-profit services, and service providers.
- Procurement negotiations aim to apply new rules to services, potentially including health services, and if applied could also lead to privatization.
- Electronic commerce negotiations, if they apply GATS national-treatment, market-access and domestic-regulation rules, could be a back door to commercializing electronic health services without Canada making any specific direct commitments to open up health services.
- The successful application of GATS rules to electronic commerce will undermine the positive potential of telehealth and telemedicine in the North.

B. NAFTA

NAFTA also contains provisions that potentially affect health care and health services in the North. Of particular concern is the potential application of NAFTA's investment provisions to health measures — that is, any government activity. At the present time, health measures of territorial and Aboriginal governments are potentially subject to challenges by individual investors through NAFTA dispute processes.

There is no *a priori* exclusion of health measures in NAFTA's investment chapter. The federal government claims that health care is protected because of a broad reservation. The reservation states:

Canada reserves the right to adopt or maintain any measure with respect to the provision of... the following services to the extent that they are social services established or maintained for a public purpose: income security or insurance, social security or insurance, social welfare, public education, public training, health, and child care.[21]

The phrases "social services" and "for a public purpose" are not defined in the agreement, and their meaning is not at all clear. If a service is delivered privately, is it still a social service as defined above? Is a private health service delivered for a fee a public service?

While this language could be used to narrow the application of the reservation, the precise meaning and its limitations will remain unclear until a trade-dispute panel provides an interpretation. Once again, the fate of our health-care system could lie in the hands of a commercial arbitration panel.

In the best-case scenario, the Canadian social-services reservation would include all possible health-care measures, even if they were provided privately for fees. Would our NAFTA reservation provide full protection for health care in Canada?

Listed in the annex to this report are all of the NAFTA articles that are excluded from application to health care. The most important exclusion of NAFTA's investment provisions is national treatment. Given the powerful impact that national treatment could have if applied to health-care measures, it is important that it be excluded.

The biggest deficit of Canada's social-services reservation is its failure to exclude the expropriation and mandatory compensation rule (NAFTA Article 1110) from application to health care (and the other listed social services). In the examination of NAFTA Article 1110 in Section 3.C.iii, it was noted that:

> At the present time, health measures of territorial and Aboriginal governments are potentially subject to challenges by individual investors through NAFTA dispute processes.

- it applies even if there is no violation of national treatment;
- it applies even if a government is acting for a public purpose; and
- compensation is mandatory if an investment is expropriated.

All of these elements of NAFTA Article 1110 appear to seriously undermine the value of Canada's broad reservation of social services. It is unclear whether or not the reservation provides any meaningful protection against an investor challenge of a health-care measure by a government in Canada.

To the extent that Canada's Medicare system does not privatize and/or allow access to foreign investors, it will be able to minimize future potential claims. If, on the other hand, privatization of health care is increased, then there is a much greater likelihood that Canada will face an investor-state dispute based on its health-care measures.

Negotiations on the larger Free Trade Agreement of the Americas (FTAA) represent a potential expansion of NAFTA investment provisions to 34 Central and Latin American nations. While the U.S. is likely the source of most challenges to Canadian measures, the expansion will only increase the risk of challenges of health-care measures. If a European-based investor operates out of one of the FTAA states, then that investor will acquire rights under the FTAA's investment provisions and could challenge Canadian health-care measures. Furthermore, the successful expansion of NAFTA-like investment provisions is a stepping stone to including these prohibitive rules in the WTO sometime in the future.

In summary:

- NAFTA's investment provisions represent a serious threat to the continuation of Canada's public health-care system.
- The Annex II reservation that the Canadian government alleges protects health care is unlikely to provide a level of protection that Canadians want.
- The Annex II reservation does not restrict the use of Article 1110 on expropriation and compensation, which represents the most serious threat to health care under NAFTA rules.
- The expansion of NAFTA-like investment provisions in the FTAA negotiations will increase the risk of investor challenges of Canada's health-care system.
- The expansion of NAFTA-like investment provisions in the FTAA is a stepping stone to the introduction of similar rules in the WTO sometime in the future.

3.   Economic Development

Since government expenditures are the single most important economic sector in the territories, there is an understandable desire to achieve greater economic diversification through the expansion of the private-sector economy. Aboriginal governments are focused on ways of increasing economic activity and employment opportunities in their communities in a manner that is consistent with their cultures.

Strategies for achieving greater economic diversification have relied on a variety of methods, including: aid for local businesses, either through preferential procurement policies or various subsidies; encouraging local economic spin-offs and value-added activity in the development and operation of natural-resource extraction; development of infrastructure that is either an economic engine in itself (such as energy) and/or is a means for facilitating economic development, such as transportation, postal services, energy, and telecommunications.

We will consider the potential impact of trade and investment treaties on three approaches to economic diversification:

A. Preferential-treatment policies

B. Value-added and spin-off policies

C. Infrastructure support

Two important caveats need to be factored into the analysis: first, the potential legal obligations of trade treaties are only relevant when there is likelihood that public policies could affect economic interests in other jurisdictions (is there a motivated nation or investor to challenge a policy?); second, trade treaties are constantly changing to decrease government latitude and increase market activity. It is important to consider future trends in trade policies and how they might affect economic policy setting in the future.

A. PREFERENTIAL-TREATMENT POLICIES

Preferential-treatment policies are common in the territories, as they are throughout Canada. For example, the NWT as of 1997 had a business-incentive policy that provided preferences to northern businesses in the tendering of procurement contracts by all governments in the NWT, as well as by organizations that receive 51 per cent or more funding from the territorial government.

The purpose of the policy was "to provide existing northern business with a level of business incentive that compensates for the higher cost of operating a business in the Northwest Territories. The business incentive will allow for northern business to compete successfully with southern business."[22] In addition, the policy is designed to help new businesses become viable, create local employment, and train administrators and managers.

In the tendering of contracts for goods, services and construction, the NWT government provides incentives for NWT businesses. This means that in the tender competition the value of the goods, services or construction is reduced by 15-20 per cent for northern content for projects over $1,000. While the price of goods, services or construction is not the sole determinant in a contract, it often is one of the most important factors used to select the successful bidder.

Nunavut has introduced a contracting policy (NNI – Nunavummi Nangminiqatunit Ikajutiit) that assesses bid adjustments for contractors, with different preferences given for local ownership, Inuit ownership, local employment, Inuit employment, and training.

The Yukon and NWT governments (but not Nunavut) are bound by procurement rules in Canada's Agreement on Internal Trade (AIT). The AIT procurement rules in Chapter 5 are similar to those used in the North American Free Trade Agreement (NAFTA) procurement rules in Chapter 10. These rules include:

- a non-discrimination clause requiring goods, services and their suppliers from anywhere in Canada to receive ". . . treatment no less favourable than the best treatment it accords to its own… " such goods, services and suppliers of goods and services;[23]
- application to procurement contracts for goods of $25,000 or more, for services of $100,000 or more and for construction of $100,000 or more;[24]
- strict rules that apply to procurement procedures;[25]
- procedures to allow a business to challenge a procurement decision;[26]
- transparency, information and reporting requirements; and
- obligations to engage in future negotiations in order to expand the coverage of the agreement to other levels of government or to public sector entities as well as to increase the applicable rules.

The procurement rules under the AIT do not apply below these thresholds, which are greater than much of the procurement undertaken in the North. However, large projects, while fewer in number, represent a major economic development opportunity and would fall under procurement rules. *Any procurement rules providing incentives to local content and their businesses would be violations of AIT procurement rules, in particular the geographic non-discrimination rule.*

The AIT procurement rules have an exemption for regional and economic-development programs. But these programs are only to be used under exceptional circumstances and must meet strict tests laid out in the agreement.[27] The bigger the procurement, the more likely it will be challenged by another territory or province. In addition, parties must list all of their regional and economic development programs they intend to use for the purposes of this exception. Another purpose of the list is for the parties to be able to negotiate a reduction of such programs and policies in the future. The ultimate goal is to have the rules apply without such exceptions.

At the present time, the AIT does not have a binding dispute-resolution process. This may well change in the future if the federal government is successful in pushing for a binding agreement. In addition, procurement negotiations are taking place at the World Trade Organization (WTO). NAFTA Article 1024 calls for negotiations to include sub-national government procurement. Finally, the negotiations to expand NAFTA into the Free Trade Area of the Americas (FTAA) will also include NAFTA-like procurement negotiations that could eventually cover sub-national governments.

In summary, the preferential-procurement policies of the northern territories:

- violate procurement rules in the AIT, to which Yukon and the NWT are signatories;
- are unlikely to be able to use the AIT regional economic-development exclusion;
- may be subject to a binding dispute process in the future, though the AIT does not yet have one; and
- could be subject to international procurement rules under the WTO, NAFTA, and the FTAA in the foreseeable future.

B. VALUE-ADDED AND SPIN-OFF POLICIES

Value-added policies are designed to leverage local economic benefits in exchange for allowing access to markets or resources for investors. For resource extraction, value-added activities are achieved through the granting of licenses. The objective is to ensure more local processing of resources as a source of more jobs, business, and other economic benefits.

There are passive value-added policies that prohibit the export of unprocessed natural resources, such as Canada's ban on raw-log exports. Other policies are more active and call for guarantees that resources will be processed in the territory of their extraction. Canada's export ban on raw logs has the added advantage of being excluded from some trade rules.[28] New value-added policies cannot realistically gain access to such exclusions.

Diamond mining is an important new economic opportunity in the North. But currently only 10-15 per cent of diamonds that come from Canadian mines are being cut and finished here[38]. Canadian diamonds now carry a premium as a result of their very high quality and because they are untainted by the controversy over diamonds from some African countries where they are used to buy arms to support military dictators and terrorists.

The present definition of a Canadian diamond is one that is mined in Canada. The NWT has asked the federal government to provide a new definition that requires a Canadian diamond to be one that is mined, cut and polished in Canada. The international industry is opposed to the new definition because the companies want to be able to process the diamonds in places like India and China, whose lower operating costs, especially labour, ensure higher profit margins.

The federal Competition Bureau is resisting demands for the new definition that the NWT government wants. One reason for that reluctance may be the pressure being exerted by the industry. Another reason that has not been stated publicly could be the concern about the proposed "value-added" definition for Canadian diamonds conflicting with Canada's international trade-treaty obligations.

Canada's export ban on raw logs has the added advantage of being excluded from some trade rules.[28] New value-added policies cannot realistically gain access to such exclusions.

One possible challenge could arise under the WTO GATS agreement. Canada has made a GATS commitment in mining services, which may possibly include services related to the cutting and processing of diamonds. Canada's entry applies to "services incidental to mining, including drilling and field services and rental of equipment with operator."[29] The labelling definition could come into conflict with this commitment, if it results in less favourable treatment for foreign mining service operators or restricts their access to the Canadian market.

Impact and benefits agreements (IBAs) are a common instrument used by both territorial and Aboriginal governments throughout the North. These agreements are used to address socio-economic, environmental, and other impacts and to ensure local and regional economic benefits when mineral development occurs in the North.[30]

The Nunavut Land Claims Agreement (NCLA) requires the use of IBAs for any large project involving the development or exploitation of resources under Inuit-owned lands. Projects involving at least 200 person-years of employment or $35 million of capital costs over five years require an IBA.

IBAs require economic benefits to accrue to Inuit peoples. These requirements include training, preferential hiring, business-development opportunities, and a number of other issues.

The dollar and employment thresholds for the application of IBAs are large enough to capture major foreign investors, as is the case for the diamond mines. Foreign investors will be aware of trade and investment rules and will use them, or lobby their governments to act on their behalf, if it is in their interests to do so.

NAFTA's Article 1106 (performance requirements) prohibits the imposition and enforcement of local benefits, including the following:

(b) to achieve a given level or percentage of domestic content;

(c) to purchase, use, or accord a preference to goods produced or services provided in its territory, or to purchase goods or services from persons in its territory;"[31]

If these prohibitions were to be followed, they could stop governments from requiring the purchase of goods or services from local businesses. With respect to the proposed new definition of a Canadian diamond, it could run afoul of NAFTA's prohibitions requiring a given level or percentage of domestic content under Article 1106 1(b), depending upon how it was implemented and enforced.

There are additional prohibitions under NAFTA Article 1106, including limits on technology transfers, a production process or other proprietary knowledge, that could limit economic development initiatives using IBAs or other economic development instruments.

The Yukon and NWT have access to Annex I reservations which would provide a degree of protection for IBAs. Aboriginal governments could have the additional protection provided by Annex II reservations. In addition, IBAs that are voluntarily negotiated with foreign firms of NAFTA parties and not enforced by the governments involved likely wouldn't violate NAFTA rules.

There are limitations to both Annex I and Annex II reservations (for example, Annex I and Annex II reservations do not prohibit a challenge under NAFTA Article 1110 (Expropriation and Compensation), which could undermine the bargaining power of governments in negotiations with foreign investors from NAFTA nations. Nonetheless, to the extent that the reservations apply, they do provide territorial and Aboriginal governments some protection for IBAs from investor-state disputes.

It is less likely that foreign investors will resort to using trade rules in the negotiations phase.[32] Unless investors have alternative jurisdictions within which they can access the same resources, they will be prepared to negotiate local economic benefits for access to profitable mines. While trade and investment challenges can occur at this stage, challenges are more likely to occur once the mine is in operation and new requirements are imposed.

The Nunavut agreement includes a role for the federal Minister of Indian and Northern Affairs Canada (INAC) to block a federal license for resource extraction if the IBA fails to meet the NCLA requirements. The role provided for the federal INAC minister could affect the potential impact that NAFTA and WTO rules have on IBAs. If a federal minister has a role to play in the IBA process, then it is likely that trade-dispute panels will view his participation as a federal measure. If that is the case, then the test for the national-treatment rule will be based on the best available treatment provided in Canada by the federal government.

If a federal license for resource extraction on Inuit-owned lands were granted without an IBA, or without adequate benefits, it could become the best treatment available in the national treatment test. The result could undermine the basic IBA's goal of achieving local economic benefits for Inuit peoples under the Nunavut agreement. However, these adverse impacts may be mitigated by the Annex II reservation for Aboriginal measures (*see above*).

The land-claims and self-government agreements in the Yukon do not require IBAs. However, there is a requirement under the Umbrella Final Agreement (UFA) to examine environmental and socio-economic impacts and mitigation measures.[33] This provision allows negotiations to focus on securing local benefits.

The federal government itself does not require IBAs to be negotiated, and there are no standard policy guidelines in place for such negotiations. At the same time, a 1999 review of IBA policy has noted that INAC ". . . appears both unwilling and unable to remove itself completely from the IBA process."[34] This ambiguity may create an uncertain atmosphere for IBAs, but it also allows them to be construed as federal measures and therefore made subject to NAFTA trade challenges.

International trade-treaty obligations can also adversely affect Aboriginal involvement in the IBA process. If Aboriginal peoples negotiate IBAs prior to the resolution of land claims, then their actions likely remain under the jurisdiction of the federal government. If Aboriginal involvement is as a result of having acquired authority over lands and mineral rights, then their actions are those of a sub-national government. If IBAs negotiated by Aboriginal peoples fall under federal jurisdiction, then the best national treatment likely will be applied at the federal level. It remains unclear if the best treatment test will apply to IBAs negotiated by or for Aboriginal peoples, or if the test will be even broader and apply to any federally negotiated IBA. Arguments could be made to justify either interpretation.

Future trade-treaty obligations are likely to further constrain efforts by northern governments to leverage local economic benefits. For example, the FTAA negotiations are currently engaged in a process of taking the most restrictive investment rules contained in NAFTA and combining them with the most restrictive services rules in the GATS. This combination does not yet exist at the multilateral level through the WTO. If the FTAA negotiations are successful, then this will be a major step towards introducing NAFTA-like investment rules, including an investor-state dispute process, into the WTO, extending the scope of such rules from just three countries (Canada, the U.S. and Mexico) to the 146 in the WTO. This would greatly increase the risk of investor-state challenges against IBAs and other value-added polices used in the North.

> Future trade-treaty obligations are likely to further constrain efforts by northern governments to leverage local economic benefits.

In summary, value-added policies:

- are potentially inconsistent with NAFTA's investment provisions and are subject to both investor and state challenges;
- are inconsistent with WTO services rules, due to unlimited commitments made by the federal government in its GATS schedule of specific commitments for several mining services;
- in the specific case of diamonds, could brake NWT efforts to get the federal government to change the definition of a Canadian diamond, due to Canada's commitment to both NAFTA and WTO rules;
- in the case of IBAs, are inconsistent with international trade-treaty rules noted above;
- in the case of the Nunavut land-claim agreement, the role for the federal minister could make IBAs federal measures subjecting them to a "best-in-country" national treatment standard;

- the ambiguous and inconsistent federal role for IBAs in the North could lead to greater risk and exposure under international trade treaties due to national-treatment rules being applied at the federal level;
- NAFTA reservations and GATS limitations provide some protection for measures related to aboriginal peoples, although the precise scope of this protection is unclear; and
- could be even further limited by continuing negotiations to expand the application of trade rules to more areas of government authority, to develop more restrictive rules and to cover more nations, increasing the risk of successful challenges of value-added initiatives, including IBAs, in the future.

4.   Infrastructure

Infrastructure in the North presents special challenges arising from low population density, large distances between communities, large distances from sources of essential goods and services (food, energy, equipment, health care, etc.), lack of year-round ground transportation in many cases, and a harsh winter climate. Northern communities could not survive in their present state, much less compete in the future, without having affordable and effective energy, transportation, and communication systems. Some infrastructure services, such as air transportation, are more essential as well, due to a lack of available alternatives. In all instances, the role of the public sector is critical, since there is little likelihood that the private sector could provide most of these infrastructure services at affordable prices for consumers without support.

Postal services are an essential part of northern life, an important source for transporting food supplies to remote communities. Air services are critical for these communities since many are without access to other forms of transportation, including road and marine transport.[35] Almost three-quarters of Canada's land mass is situated in the North and includes the Yukon, the NWT, and Nunavut, as well as the northern parts of most provinces. The total population of these areas is more than 260,000 people (1996 census), served by Canada Post in 257 northern communities.[36]

Canada Post Corporation has a broad mandate: "(a) to establish and operate a postal service for the collection, transmission and delivery of messages, information, funds and goods both within Canada and places outside Canada."[37] Its mandate also includes: "(b) the need to conduct its operations on a self-sustaining financial basis while providing a standard of service that will meet the needs of the people of Canada and that is similar with respect to communities of the same size."[38]

Canada Post delivers letters anywhere in the country for the same rate, ensuring that people in the three territories have the same service for the same price as do people in densely populated communities in the south. Canada Post has a virtual monopoly for letter services, with some limited exceptions.[39]

Delivery rates and other important issues, including environmental considerations for unaddressed advertising mail, are all controlled by the federal cabinet. Such political oversight ensures that non-commercial values are also taken into consideration in the operation of postal services.

Canada Post also delivers a surplus back to the government each year. Most recently, Canada Post paid a dividend of approximately $21 million to the federal government, in addition to over $80 million in income taxes.[40]

Northbound mail is made up mostly of parcels and food. Canada Post estimated that operating costs for its northern services division were $66 million, compared to revenues of only $17 million (1998-99). Even with INAC contributing subsidies of $16 million, Canada Post lost $33 million in its northern postal services division. *In other words, postage rates in the North would have to triple in order to cover the cost of service.*

Canada Post is also involved in courier services, having bought 94 per cent of Purolator Courier. Purolator competes with private courier companies such as United Parcel Services (UPS), a U.S.-based multinational company. UPS is the largest express carrier and package-delivery company in the world, operating in more than 200 countries and territories. Its estimated value is more than US$67 billion, its revenues for 2002 were more than US$31 billion, and it employs about 360,000 people.[41] Canada Post revenues for 2001 were about US$4 billion, and it has about 66,000 employees.

In spite of UPS's dominance on a global scale, Canada Post controls more than 50 per cent of the domestic courier business in Canada. In an effort to increase their market share, UPS and other private courier companies brought two cases against Canada Post before the Competition Bureau, arguing that Purolator is being cross-subsidized by Canada Post's letter-mail infrastructure. Both cases failed for lack of evidence of cross-subsidization.

NAFTA provided UPS with another method for attacking Canada Post's courier services. UPS filed a "notice of intent to submit a claim to arbitration" under NAFTA's provisions for investors to challenge governments. UPS is making similar arguments to those made in its failed domestic Competition Bureau cases, but is packaging them within NAFTA rules, alleging that Canada Post violated competition and national-treatment rules. UPS is claiming not less than US$100 million as compensation for damages.[42]

If it is found to be in violation of NAFTA rules, Canada Post will end up paying damages as well as facing more pressure to increase access to the courier-services market by private courier services – the main objective of UPS and the private courier industry. This could diminish Canada Post's revenues and challenge its financial independence from taxpayers. Since Canada Post has an obligation to operate on a self-sustaining financial basis, this could result in increased costs for consumers. Such cost increases would weigh disproportionately on the North because of the heavy reliance on postal services for food and other essential goods.

The General Agreement on Trade in Services (GATS) represents another trade treaty that global courier corporations could use to challenge Canada Post's public-service role. The GATS covers all actions of a state, including its public corporations. As described in Section 3, the GATS contains an exclusion for services delivered in the exercise of governmental authority. The two-fold test requires that such services be delivered without competition and not be commercial in nature.

Canada Post courier services are clearly not excluded because they are in direct competition with private courier services. Most Canada Post letter-mail services are delivered as a monopoly and without competition. However, would Canada Post letter-mail services be commercial? The service is provided for a fee, and Canada Post has a mandate to operate in a financially independent manner. Canada Post also pays taxes and returns a dividend to the federal government. Would these factors in combination lead a WTO dispute panel to conclude that Canada Post is a commercial operation? Canada Post also has a broader public mandate, such as providing services to the North at a loss. Would this role render it non-commercial?

There is no definition of "commercial" in the GATS, and that makes it difficult to predict how a WTO trade-dispute panel would rule on this matter. Also, the government-authority exclusion does not apply if Canada makes commitments for these services under GATS specific rules.

The two primary and most powerful GATS rules are national treatment and market access. These are rules (to which Canada has made specific commitments for courier services) that are broad and contain few limitations. Courier services are defined as those that provide the delivery of letters, parcels and packages by a provider other than a national postal administration. Canada has not yet made similar commitments for postal services or mail transportation by air.[43] Postal services include the delivery of letters, parcels and packages by a national postal administration.

How would the national treatment rule be applied to courier services in Canada? If Purolator is not considered to be an operation within a national postal administration by a trade panel, then foreign courier services are entitled to the best treatment that Purolator receives from Canada Post. This likely would force Canada Post out of the courier business.

On the other hand, since Purolator is considered to be part of the national postal administration, National Treatment would require a government to provide a foreign courier service the best treatment available to private domestic companies. The final interpretation of how national treatment applies to Canadian commitments under courier services can only be made by a WTO trade-dispute panel.

GATS market-access provisions are absolute and apply regardless of whether or not there is a national-treatment violation. Market-access provisions prohibit two types of government measures: those that limit the form of ownership (public ownership over private ownership, for example) and those that establish quotas, limits, or other quantitative restrictions on a company's operations.

If it is found to be in violation of NAFTA, Canada Post will end up paying damages and facing pressure to increase access to the courier-services market. Resulting cost increases would weigh disproportionately on the North because of the heavy reliance on postal services for food and other essential goods.

If GATS prohibitions against quantitative restrictions were to apply to postal services, Canada could not require courier services to have a minimum number of outlets, depots, counter services or offices in northern communities. If the private courier industry were able to force Canada Post to withdraw from courier services, Canada could not require the private sector to provide equivalent postal services in the North and remain consistent with its GATS obligations.

Northern postal services are now run at a loss. If private firms were to enter the market, they are likely to increase prices, lower the quality of services, and/or provide fewer services in order to become profitable. Addressing this prospect in a national review of Canada Post, the National Farmers' Union noted:

> *Courier competition has brought few benefits to rural and remote areas. Currently, many rural residents cannot get home delivery of courier packages, and there is no local location for parcel pick-up. As of 1989, there were many regions that did not have access to courier service, other than provided by Canada Post. Even large centres such as Grande Prairie, Alberta, did not have full courier service. Canada Post is the only provider of courier services which can be accessed by all Canadians.*[44]

This scenario is based on the application of the existing GATS rules to Canada Post and Purolator. But the GATS is presently being re-negotiated in Geneva. There are three possible routes to expanding GATS coverage over Canada Post operations:

1. Efforts are being made to increase services that are covered by all GATS rules, including demands for Canada to make commitments in courier services and air services.

2. Efforts are being made to alter the classification system, so that the distinction between postal services (delivered by a national postal administration) and courier services (delivered outside of the national postal administration) would be eliminated. If successful, Canada's current commitment in courier services could fully capture Canada Post courier services.

3. Efforts are being made to develop additional market limits that could capture all or part of Canada Post's operations, including electronic communication. This could cut off areas of future growth and future sources of revenues for Canada Post.

If these negotiations result in the approval of the proposed rules in any one of the above areas, this will open up the Canadian market for courier and other postal services to the private sector at the expense of Canada Post and its broad public mandate. While most Canadians will suffer from the lost of yet another national institution, northerners will suffer even more.

In summary:

- Postal services are a key part of the social and economic fabric of northern communities, which are more reliant on postal services than other parts of Canada.
- Costs for northern postal services are three times as high as revenues, exceeding revenues by about $33 million, plus $16 million in INAC subsidies.
- Canada Post is now being challenged by UPS under a NAFTA investor dispute, which, if successful, could result in high compensation costs for the federal government (more than US$100 million is being requested) and also lead to more privatized postal services in Canada.
- The GATS in its present form represents a potential avenue for global courier corporations to challenge public postal services and lead to their greater privatization.
- The present negotiations have the potential to expand the coverage of GATS rules over Canadian postal services and increase the risk of deregulation and privatization.
- The North is more likely to be adversely affected by privatized postal services, which will need to increase prices, reduce quality of services, and/or reduce the amounts and locations of services in order to operate on a profitable basis.

5.   Environment

A. ENVIRONMENTAL CHALLENGES AND GOVERNMENT MEASURES

Humans have inhabited the Arctic for thousands of years, living by fishing, hunting, and gathering. Many of the peoples living in the Arctic are still greatly dependent on living resources for their livelihood. Today, man not only uses the living resources but has also to a great extent explored and developed non-renewable resources like oil, gas, minerals, and metals. These conditions have severe impacts on the species of the Arctic. Habitat fragmentation, climate change, pollution and overexploitation all affect the flora and fauna. Finding a balance between commercial development and conservation issues is a huge challenge.[45]

Canada is one of eight nations that participate in the Arctic Council, an international body that seeks joint solutions to common concerns. The main challenge, as noted above, is to find a balance between commercial developments and respect for the environment, traditional cultures and human health.

While indigenous peoples continue fishing, hunting and gathering, it is becoming increasingly difficult to sustain this way of life. Commercial exploitation of natural resources has brought non-Aboriginal peoples to live and work in the North on major projects that have also increased the presence and role of non-aboriginal governments. These developments have acted to "push" Aboriginal people off of their land and out of their traditional economic base, as well as to "pull" them into a new commercial economy.

Activities such as mining and petroleum have resulted in disturbance, loss and fragmentation of the habitat, threatening biodiversity. Road construction, pipelines, mining activities and logging are the main sources of environmental degradation. The Arctic Council estimates that, in the first half of the 20th century only 5 per cent of the Arctic was affected by infrastructure developments. In the second half of the century, the areas affected grew to 25 per cent. The projections for the future show that affected areas could double.[46]

i. Domestic Environmental-Protection Measures

In response to an increasing awareness of the risks associated with contaminated sites, the Yukon government in 1996 passed stricter regulations to control them, including this definition of such a site:

> *A contaminated site is one deemed unsuitable for its intended use because of toxic substances left behind by commercial or industrial activities. Some examples of such toxins are PCBs, heavy metals, and hydrocarbons. There are several hundred contaminated sites of varying size and complexity in the Yukon.*[47]

The regulations allow the government to determine if the site is hazardous and who is responsible and to require restoration if necessary.

The regulations are based on the Yukon's 1991 *Environment Act*, which is a broad instrument designed to allow the government and its citizens rights to "… a healthful natural environment."[48] The Act provides for the right of action by every adult or corporation resident in the Yukon who has reasonable grounds to believe that someone has impaired or is likely to impair the environment, or that the Yukon government has failed to meet its obligations to protect the environment.[49]

If a corporation impairs the environment as noted above, then the Yukon Supreme Court has the right to grant an injunction to stop the operation of such a commercial activity and award damages as well as costs. In addition, the court can also order a company found guilty of polluting the environment to restore or rehabilitate any part of the natural environment, and can suspend or cancel a permit, among other measures.[50]

Of particular interest is the relationship of the Yukon's *Environmental Act* to Aboriginal land-claim and self-government agreements. Article 3 of the Act makes it clear that, in the event of a conflict between land-claim agreements and/or self-government agreements and the Act, ". . . the land-claims agreement or the self-government agreement shall prevail to the extent of the conflict." This ensures that First Nations in the Yukon have a degree of control over issues that could affect their traditional culture and way of life. These traditional lifestyles are generally less commercial in nature and have a more sustainable relationship to the land and Nature. This allows for a much greater emphasis on environmental and health protection than might otherwise occur in non-Aboriginal settings.

Activities such as mining and petroleum have resulted in disturbance, loss and fragmentation of the habitat, threatening biodiversity.

In summary:

- The North is a fragile environment that is being exposed to challenges arising out of resource development, including major infrastructure that can harm lands and animal and plant life.
- Territorial governments have developed environmental-protection legislation and regulations that are designed to achieve a balance between much-needed economic development and protection of the environment.
- Aboriginal governments and their peoples face great challenges in trying to maintain traditional lifestyles and protect the environment while searching for new economic opportunities.

ii. Global Environmental Issues

The degradation of the fragile northern environment is not solely based on commercial exploitation of northern resources. Other regions of the world export a number of environmental problems to the North:

- Climate change is taking place in the North with strong, variable, and unpredictable effects on Nature (habitat and wildlife) and communities. The biggest temperature increases from global warming are predicted to take place in the Arctic. Dramatic increases in average temperature have already been observed, accompanied by thinning ice levels and reduced ice cover. Thawing of the permafrost and reduction of ozone are the potential impacts. Global warming caused from greenhouse gas emissions in industrial and industrializing nations is the major cause of climate change.

- Long-range transportation effects from other parts of North America and beyond are another source of environmental stress for the North. The Arctic is a sink for global pollution because of the flow of oceanic and atmospheric currents. There are a variety of pollutants affecting the Arctic, the most important of which include:

  - persistent organic pollutants (POPs), industrial and agricultural chemicals transported by the atmosphere and found in high concentrations in the Arctic; POPs include DDT, PCBs and lindane, among other cancer-generating agents; and

  - heavy metals such as mercury and lead, known carcinogens that are found in high concentrations in the Arctic and associated with brain damage among infants and young children.

Both POPs and heavy metals tend to concentrate in the fish and game that are part of traditional diets. The result is that the indigenous peoples in the North are exposed to higher levels of these materials than the general population in Canada. These higher levels of environmental toxins are believed to be factors in the poorer health status of indigenous peoples.

The Stockholm Convention is a global treaty to protect human health and the environment from persistent organic pollutants (POPs). POPs are chemicals that remain intact in the environment for long periods, become widely distributed geographically, accumulate in the fatty tissue of living organisms, and are toxic to humans and wildlife. POPs circulate globally and can cause damage wherever they travel. In implementing the convention, governments will take measures to eliminate or reduce the release of POPs into the environment.[51]

The Stockholm Convention represents a major step forward in the effort to eliminate or reduce the production, use, and export of POPs.

The Kyoto Protocol is an international agreement designed to deal with climate change by reducing greenhouse-gas emissions. Greenhouse gases are those generated mainly through the burning of fossil fuels such as coal and oil. Scientists predict that the higher levels of greenhouse gases will cause a significant warming of the Earth by about one to five degrees Celsius. Without a global reduction of greenhouse gases, climate change will produce disastrous changes to the environment, including the melting of ice caps in the Arctic.

Kyoto commits industrialized nations to cut their greenhouse-gas emissions to a level that is 5.2 per cent below the 1990 level and is to be achieved between the years 2008-2012. The U.S. has not ratified the Kyoto Protocol, but Canada has. This has generated a storm of controversy in Canada, since it is assumed that reducing greenhouse-gas emissions will be an economic disadvantage for Canada and an economic advantage for the U.S. While such assumptions may not turn out to be accurate, they reflect short-run and narrow commercial views of the economy by parts of the business community.

For the North, the main issue is the long-term sustainability of the environment and of indigenous cultures, as well as the health and well-being of northerners in general. While extreme commercial views tend to exclude the environment and labour from the economy, most Canadians, and northerners in particular, cannot afford to adopt such a myopic perspective.

In summary:

- The North is the recipient and depository of some of the most dangerous agricultural and industrial chemicals produced and used in major industrial nations.
- Serious harm is being caused to the environment and health of northern peoples, especially Aboriginal peoples who subsist on a traditional fishing, hunting and gathering economy.
- The North is also experiencing a disproportionate impact caused by global warming that could harm both its ecology and its economy.
- The Stockholm Convention on POPs and the Kyoto Protocol are major international steps to control some of these environmental problems and, if properly implemented and enforced, will help protect the North from further environmental degradation.

B. IMPACTS OF TRADE TREATIES

There are two types of measures that governments have undertaken to deal with environmental protection. The first is domestic measures, such as the Yukon *Environment Act,* that are designed to deal with environmental issues arising from economic activity within the territory. The second is international agreements, such as the Kyoto Protocol on greenhouse gases. How are government measures such as these likely to be affected by international trade agreements?

i. Domestic Environmental Measures

Environmental values and measures do have some degree of protection within trade treaties. But are these protections adequate to allow territorial and Aboriginal governments to protect the environment according to their own values and needs?

As cited frequently in earlier sections, both WTO and NAFTA rules give market access and commercial values priority status over all others. The environment and human health are relegated to the status of being "exceptions" to these commercial values. Environmental values can be used to justify measures, but not solely at the discretion of the government involved. Rather, environmental protection measures must meet market and trade access tests.

a. WTO Exceptions for Domestic Environment Measures

As previously mentioned, there is only one case where a government successfully used an exception for human health in a trade panel ruling under the WTO (an asbestos case brought by Canada against France). There are no WTO cases where a government has successfully used an exception for environmental measures to defend an otherwise non-conforming measure.

The general exception in the GATT 1994 (the WTO agreement dealing with goods) allows for the protection of measures necessary to protect human, animal or plant life health. In addition, governments are allowed to take measures relating to the conservation of an exhaustible natural resource, as long as the same measures are applied domestically.[52]

Trade panels have interpreted the GATT Article XX on general exceptions in the following ways:

- Exceptions must be interpreted narrowly, as their purpose is to permit measures that otherwise violate GATT rules.

- Exceptions must not undermine the basic objectives and principles of the GATT, which is to open markets and trade in goods.
- The burden of proof is placed on the government using the exception to show that the measure in question is the least trade-restrictive option necessary to achieve the environmental policy aim.
- "Necessary" to protect human, animal or plant life means "indispensable," "requisite," "inevitably determined," or "unavoidable."[53]
- Since "necessary" means "unavoidable," consideration must be given to alternative measures that are reasonably available, and the one chosen must be the least inconsistent with GATT rules.
- Measures cannot be an arbitrary or unjustifiable discrimination between nations, nor can they be disguised restrictions on trade.
- Mandatory measures that require actions violating GATT rules can be found to be a violation of the GATT even if they have not yet been invoked.[54]
- Any restrictions on the use of a natural resource for conservation reasons must be applied domestically as well as to other WTO member nations.

There is only one case where a government successfully used an exception for human health in a trade panel ruling under the WTO; there are no cases for environmental measures.

The main vulnerabilities for environmental and health measures occur when the relevant science is not definitive and the body of available research is in its early stages of development. This is precisely when governments will want to use the precautionary principle and stop or delay potentially harmful commercial activity. The industry response to the health threats created by asbestos is a case in point.

> When OSHA (the U.S. Occupational Safety and Health Administration, Department of Labour) began hearings in 1972, the industry fought strenuously against any reduction in permissible exposure levels on the alleged grounds that the dangers of asbestos were minimal. The basis for the industry case was strongly argued by academic consultants, some from medical schools or schools of public health, some of whose research and publications were supported directly or indirectly by grants or funds from the industry or industry-financed foundations.[55]

The same principle applies to tobacco, where the industry deliberately muddied the waters by obtaining studies that contradicted the work of other scientists showing the harmful effects of tobacco. In spite of current knowledge that cigarettes are killers, a 1990 GATT trade panel was asked to rule on the suitability of trade restrictions on tobacco for the protection of human health. The dispute panel ruled that Thailand was not allowed to prohibit the imports of U.S. tobacco products even though Thailand was concerned that these products would increase smoking rates. Instead, the panel ruled that a restriction on tobacco advertising was the least trade restrictive method of achieving that country's goal.[56]

Why would a trade panel be protecting the interests of the tobacco industry or any other producers of harmful substances, such as asbestos? Why should trade in harmful substances be encouraged? Why should a government be limited in its actions to protect its citizens from a known carcinogen? Wouldn't the combination of an import restriction on U.S. cigarettes, combined with an advertising ban, prove to be more effective at restricting cigarette use? Who should make these decisions? Most citizens would want their own governments to make these decisions, and if left to their own devices would take any actions that might reduce tobacco consumption, including an import ban.

> Why should a government be limited in its actions to protect its citizens from a known carcinogen? Who should make these decisions?

The first dispute under the WTO involved an environmental-protection measure. The United States Environmental Protection Agency (EPA) was directed by Congress to develop new regulations under the *Clean Air Act* on the composition and emission effects of gasoline in order to improve air quality by reducing vehicle emissions of toxic air pollutants and ozone-forming volatile organic compounds.[57] Because of the way in which the new regulations were implemented, the international trade-dispute panel ruled that the U.S. failed to provide foreign refiners, blenders and importers the best available treatment accorded to domestic counterparts. Hence, the U.S. was found to be in violation of the national treatment rule.

> *This is to underscore the fact that the regulations at issue in this case were not established to regulate gasoline trade, nor were they created to improve the competitive position of U.S. fuel refiners. Rather, the* Clear Air Act *initiative clearly represented a* bona fide *effort to address the*

serious air quality problems caused by gasoline combustion, particularly in regions of the country suffering from significant levels of air pollution. Whatever the impacts of the Clean Air Act *regulations on foreign gas producers, it is undeniable that those effects were incidental to the environmental goals the EPA was endeavoring to achieve.*[58]

Even though the U.S. was found to be in violation of national-treatment obligations, it attempted to argue that the measure was excepted under GATT Article XX sections (b) and (g). The panel rejected the arguments because the U.S. did not demonstrate that its measures were necessary to meet its objective. The panel deemed that less trade-inconsistent alternatives were available and that these would be less costly to foreign gasoline refiners.

It is apparent that the panel was more concerned with the commercial interest of foreign enterprises than it was with the needs of protecting the environment.

The General Agreement on Trade in Services (GATS) also allows for general exceptions similar to those in the earlier, broader GATT. However, the GATS language weakens the exclusions available under the GATT in two ways.

First, there is no exclusion for exhaustible natural resources under the GATS. It may be argued that these resources are goods and only require protection under the goods agreement. However, there are services associated with the extraction of natural resources, including mining, logging, and engineering services and a host of others that could be used to challenge environmental-protection measures under GATS rules.

WTO trade panel decisions have permitted appellants to select the most advantageous agreement on which to base a trade challenge. GATS rules can be invoked even if the measure is primarily designed to apply to goods and it only incidentally affects trade in services. Dispute panels have also ruled that, in the event that both the GATT and the GATS apply, the set of rules that restricts trade the least must be used.

Second, the GATS narrows the application of measures designed to protect human, animal and plant health or life by setting a more stringent test for non-discriminatory treatment. GATT Article XX states that, in order to benefit from the general exception for human health and environmental protection, a measure cannot be applied in a manner "... which would constitute a means of arbitrary or unjustifiable discrimination between countries where *the same conditions prevail...*" GATS Article XIV changes the highlighted words to read "... where *like conditions prevail...*"

This change sets a tougher standard for non-discriminatory treatment, thereby reducing the level of protection provided by the GATS exception *(emphasis added)*.

For example, under the GATT, health rules applied to a foreign-owned gold mine can be different than rules applied to a domestic-owned diamond mine because they would not cover the same conditions. Hence, higher standards to protect human, animal and plant health or life are permissible for use in a gold mine even though it is foreign-owned.

The GATS allows for the possibility that gold mines and diamond mines operate under "like" conditions. The test for "like" could mean that, while the end product is different, the conditions for extracting the product are similar. In this example, both gold and diamonds are mined and this could be the basis for "like" conditions. If they are "like," they both may have to be provided the same level of treatment, even though environmental impacts differ.

In this way, the GATS increases the protection provided to trade and commercial interests and reduces the available environmental protection. The Canadian Environmental Law Association (CELA) has noted, ". . . environmental measures need to be ecosystem-specific, with protections designed to comply with unique ecological characteristics."[59] The GATS moves us further away from sound environmental-protection principles.

Further GATS negotiations will serve to increase risks for domestic environmental-protection measures in several ways. First, the European Union has proposed to cluster a group of environmental services and have them covered under specific rules. Included among the environmental-services cluster are sewage and water treatment. These services would liberalize the ownership and regulatory oversight of water services – meaning that water services could be privatized and controls on the exports of bulk water could be restricted. Given the central role of water in the environment, the loss of control over water resources could be very harmful to the environment and the local economy.

Second, the application of domestic regulations to environmental measures could mean that licensing and standards for natural-resource extraction and processing, such as for mines, would be subject to international, rather than local, standards. The application of international standards to goods in other WTO agreements has approved international standards, established through the International Standards Organization (ISO), to be trade consistent.[60] The ISO is made up of industry groups, as well as government representatives. Small governments with few resources, such as territorial or Aboriginal governments, are rarely represented at ISO standards-setting meetings. This gives private industry a huge advantage over small governments such as the territories and First Nations.

Any efforts to exceed these international standards are deemed inconsistent with free trade unless proven otherwise. This means that any higher environmental standards in the North would have to meet a test of being the least trade-restrictive way of meeting their objectives. Further, these objectives would have to be supported by science, for example, proving that the North is a more fragile environment. The ability to use precaution where science cannot be definitive is very limited in WTO agreements.[61]

For Aboriginal governments, the use of traditional values to set standards would be even more difficult to achieve, especially if the standards were higher than those set by the ISO. How might trade panels view Aboriginal objectives for higher environmental standards in order to meet the need of the traditional hunting, fishing and gathering activities? Since these are not market-based economic activities, they would likely run afoul of various principles to allow freer trade.

> Further GATS negotiations will serve to increase risks for domestic environmental-protection measures in several ways.

It is safe to conclude that the expansion of the GATS could result in greater risks for environmental-protection measures from trade challenges. Water in particular is a great concern because of its critical role in a healthy environment and because of the increased demand for water that comes from the southwestern U.S. Aboriginal governments seeking a balance between the maintenance of traditional lifestyles and economic development of available natural resources could be affected by trade challenges in the future.

In summary:

- WTO agreements on goods and services treat environmental considerations as being inconsistent with their major rules unless they can be excepted.
- The exceptions provided in the WTO agreements are very narrow and have not been successfully used to defend challenges to domestic environmental measures.

- WTO agreements require that environmental protection measures pursue the least trade-restrictive option available to meet the goal, even if it is not the best option available to protect the environment.
- WTO agreements encourage the adoption of international standards (including environmental standards) set by international organizations such as the ISO, an organization that involves industry representatives, but which generally lacks representation by sub-national governments.
- Standards that exceed international standards referenced in trade agreements do not benefit from exceptions for environmental protection, and are exposed to trade rule restrictions.
- The GATS negotiations, if successful in covering domestic regulations and including environmental services under specific rules, will lead to increased risk for domestic environmental-protection measures.
- Efforts to protect water and the environment through value-added initiatives will both be exposed to increased risks to trade challenges if the GATS is expanded.

b. NAFTA and Domestic Environmental-Protection Measures

NAFTA's chapter on goods replicates most of the rules contained in the GATT, including the exceptions in Article XX sections (b) on health and (g) on resource conservation. But NAFTA goes further, with more market-opening provisions for goods that supplement the restrictions contained in the GATT. NAFTA Article 315 on other export measures adds what has become known at the "proportionality clause" — a country must continue to export goods to other countries at the same rate as it has averaged for the past three years. In addition, the prices charged internationally cannot be higher than the domestic price, except for those changes that occur as a result of changes in supply and demand.

This proportionality clause is clearly designed to ensure that the U.S. will continue to gain access to Canada's natural resources at the lowest possible price. Reductions in exports are allowed for conservation purposes if a similar reduction occurs in domestic consumption. The net effect is to deny Canada control over its own resources. Diamond mining could be affected, as could water, neither of which were excepted from these rules. If the product were exported in its raw form, then it would have to continue to be exported in this form. Any efforts made to refine the product in order to add value would change its classification, that is, make it a different product for the purposes of NAFTA.

While restrictions for protecting the exhaustion of a resource are possible, there is no exception for reductions in exports of goods or resources because of environmental degradation that occurs from, for example, the extraction of minerals. Article 315 is silent on this issue.

Furthermore, it is unclear if the proportionality requirements apply at the national level or at the sub-national level. Exports of goods that cross borders would appear to fall within federal jurisdiction. If that is the case, then it could create disputes among exporting territories and provinces if one of them chooses to restrict its output for environmental reasons. For example, if Newfoundland and Labrador cut back its water exports, could pressure be mounted to increase the exports of water from the North?

At this point, water is not being exported, and the proportionality clause may well inhibit any such actions in the future. But it is clear that NAFTA's rules on export measures could have an adverse impact on the environment of the North. U.S. market access takes priority over the northern environment as well as the northern economy.

NAFTA's investment provisions add a major threat to environmental-protection measures of territorial and aboriginal governments. In the short history of NAFTA, almost 30 per cent of all challenges by private interests against governments have involved environmental measures. Half of these environmental challenges have been mounted against Canadian measures. The total damages claimed for compensation under NAFTA for environmental challenges amounts to US$15.75 billion. However, the actual damages awarded are US$37 million, half of which were paid by the Canadian government.[62]

Canadian governments' environmental measures challenged include:

- B.C.'s *Water Protection Act* because it stopped the bulk export of water;
- federal efforts to ban the importation of a fuel additive known as "MMT" because it was a suspected neurotoxin, adversely affecting the central nervous system;
- the federal effort to ban the use of lindane, one of the POPs known to be affecting the North and a known carcinogen; and
- the temporary federal ban on the export of toxic PCBs for waste treatment.

The federal government lost the case on PCBs and agreed to settle the MMT case before a panel could rule. The lindane case is under way, while the case against water exports has not been pursued. In the MMT case, the federal government rescinded the import ban and paid a U.S. company C$20 million for damages and issued a public apology. In the case involving the PCB export ban, a NAFTA tribunal ruled that Canada had violated NAFTA investment provisions and ordered payment of C$5 million.

In a case brought by a U.S. company against the Mexican government, a dispute panel ruled that efforts made by a local government to stop the building and operation of a toxic-waste-treatment plant were a form of expropriation and ordered payment of US$16 million. In this particular case, the panel ruled on the division of powers in the Mexican constitution (as described in Section 3), namely that a national government that signs a trade treaty commits all sub-national governments in its jurisdiction.

If the federal government permitted water exports out of one Canadian territory or province, a private investor could challenge any subsequent federal prohibition on bulk water removals in other jurisdictions. There can be little doubt that NAFTA investment provisions are among the most dangerous for environmental-protection measures. The fact that the FTAA negotiations are attempting to expand the application of NAFTA investment rules to 34 nations in the Americas is troubling.

Like the WTO agreements, NAFTA also has provisions to allow for the protection of the environment. In addition to the reservation system that was discussed in Section 3 and in addition to the general exceptions (using the same language as the GATT general exceptions), NAFTA has added a new dimension to the treatment of environmental issues in trade treaties. It contains a parallel accord known as the North American Agreement on Environmental Cooperation.[63] It is called a "parallel accord" because it is not a part of the main NAFTA text. The clauses in the environmental accord do not get read into the application of any NAFTA trade and investment rules.

Here are some of the main features of this environmental accord:
- The accord does not establish base environmental standards for the three NAFTA countries, and each country is free to set its own standards (Article 3).
- Countries are expected to fully implement whatever environmental standards they may have (Article 5).

- Individual citizens and non-governmental organizations can submit evidence to the secretariat (administrative body) that a party to the agreement is not living up to its own environmental obligations (Articles 6 & 14).
- If the application is accepted by the secretariat and it meets all of the requirements, the council (decision-making body) may require that a factual record be prepared and may also require that it be made public (Article 15).
- There is also a dispute process for each country to challenge other countries party to the environmental agreement (Articles 22-36).
- The challenge must be based on a country's "persistent pattern of failure" (sustained or recurring actions or inactions) to enforce its own environmental law.
- If the case goes to a full hearing and the country is found guilty of a persistent pattern of failure to enforce its environmental law(s), then monetary damages can be awarded up to 0.007 per cent of total trade in goods between the countries (Annex 34).
- The agreement also provides for research, education, assessment and promotional activities (Article 2).

If the federal government permitted water exports out of one Canadian territory or province, a private investor could challenge any subsequent federal prohibition on bulk water removals in other jurisdictions.

The environmental accord represents a new and potentially positive step in efforts to develop a more sustainable approach to the economy. But there are several downsides to it as well:

- In the event that the environmental agreement encourages or forces a country to enforce its own environmental measures, there is nothing to preclude a foreign investor who is affected by these enforcement measures from filing a challenge and no reason for a panel to preclude ruling that the actions are forms of expropriation for which there is mandatory compensation.
- The environmental agreement exists in the context of a broader trade-liberalizing agenda, and the secretariat may not be in a position to conduct research or educational work in a fully independent manner.

- The focus on enforcement, including the use of financial penalties and public embarrassment of factual records, could be counterproductive and discourage countries from developing more stringent environmental standards.
- The application of environmental accord rules through NACEC has not led to any increased protection for the environment in any of the three NAFTA nations through laws, policies, or enforcement.

In summary:

- NAFTA's "proportionality" clause makes efforts to protect the environment even more difficult than the rules in GATT.
- Canada's water resources, including those in the North, are a potential target of trade challenges using the proportionality clause.
- If proportionality requirements are applied at the federal level, then territorial and Aboriginal governments could lose control over their water.
- NAFTA's investment provisions have already been used to successfully challenge Canadian government measures to protect the environment.
- The Canadian government lost one investor challenge and settled another case launched against it, and was forced to withdraw environmental protection measures, pay damages of C$25 million, and in one instance, publicly apologize.
- Another investor challenge in process deals with the banning of lindane, a known carcinogen and one of the chemicals that is found in higher concentrations in the North.
- The FTAA negotiations are attempting to expand the application of NAFTA into all of the Americas and, if successful, will increase potential challenges of environmental-protection measures.
- NAFTA also has a special environmental-cooperation agreement that is not a part of the main NAFTA text.
- While potentially a positive effort to enhance environmental protection, the cooperation agreement has some serious downsides that may discourage the introduction of stronger environmental-protection measures.

ii. International Environmental Agreements

It is apparent that the problems associated with issues such as global warming and persistent organic pollutants cannot be solved through domestic environmental laws alone. Multilateral environmental agreements (known as MEAs) are essential to any realistic solution for international environmental challenges. While these agreements do not replace domestic environmental-protection measures, they ensure that domestic measures reflect the need to protect the global environment.

At the same time, MEAs pose challenges because each signatory nation will have unique economic issues to manage. For example, Canada's participation in the Kyoto Protocol negotiations required the involvement of each territory and province. Each jurisdiction had economic interests to protect, and that often involved difficult negotiations to resolve the allocation of quotas, etc. It is not surprising that at the end of the day the federal government made the commitment to Kyoto without a detailed agreement by provinces and territories on their contributions. While this is not a desirable method of proceeding, it may have been necessary in this situation.

> Multilateral environmental agreements (known as MEAs) are essential to any realistic solution for international environmental challenges.

Given the enormous challenges of getting MEAs negotiated and implemented, and given the urgent nature of the issues involved, it is important to understand the relationship between these environmental agreements and trade treaties.

In "The preambular language of the Marakesh Agreement Establishing the World Trade Organization," the first paragraph states that the parties are ". . . seeking to protect and preserve the environment and to enhance the means for doing so in a manner consistent with their respective needs and concerns at different levels of economic development."[64] The parties agreed to establish the Committee on Trade and the Environment (CTE) and provide it with a very broad mandate as a method for meeting the above objective. Over the years, both the effectiveness and the objectives of the CTE have been called into doubt:

> *It is telling of the orientation of the Committee's discussions that the issues upon which most attention settled had little to do with enlarging the scope for environmental initiative in the WTO context, but rather*

with the prospects for diminishing it. For example, on the subject of MEAs, the Committee's report asserts the right of WTO members to challenge the use of trade measures taken in accordance with the provisions of an MEA to which it is actually party, under WTO dispute resolution. While few anticipated that the Committee's work would actually undermine the integrity of MEAs, this is the likely effect of its deliberations.[65]

Not surprisingly, the CTE views MEAs as being much like domestic environmental measures of member nations and must therefore conform to trade liberalization rules unless exceptional circumstances prevail. Hence, environmental protection measures taken as a result of MEAs would have to meet the necessity test within WTO rules: they must be the least trade-restrictive option available to meet the environmental objective. As noted previously, the fact that the national treatment rule is based upon "like" goods could also be used to weaken the application of environmental rules. For the same reasons, this could also weaken MEAs. These and other limitations for exceptions discussed above would make the task of implementing and enforcing MEAs more difficult.

There may be a conflict between MEAs and trade liberalization; MEAs restrict market access for dangerous goods or endangered species, whereas WTO rules expand market access. WTO rules are structured in such a manner as to ensure that the inevitable compromises arising out of this basic conflict generally occur in favour of market liberalization. If used in this manner, WTO rules could undermine the effectiveness of MEAs.

NAFTA does contain more explicit language that more clearly defines its relationship to MEAs. Of critical importance is Article 104: Relation to Environmental and Conservation Agreements:

1. In the event of any inconsistency between this Agreement and the specific trade obligations set out in:

    a. the Convention on International Trade in Endangered Species of Wild Fauna and Flora, *done at Washington, March 3, 1973, as amended June 22, 1979;*

    b. the Montreal Protocol on Substances that Deplete the Ozone Layer, *done at Montreal, September 16, 1987, as amended June 29 1990;*

    c. the Basel Convention on the Control of Transboundary Movements of Hazardous Wastes and their Disposal, *done at Basel, March 22, 1989, on its entry into force for Canada, Mexico and the United States; or*

> d. *the agreements set out in Annex 104.1 (Bilateral and Other Environmental and Conservation Agreements),*
>
> *such obligations shall prevail to the extent of the inconsistency, provided that where the Party has choice among equally effective and reasonably available means of complying with such obligations, the Party chooses the alternative that is the least inconsistent with the other provisions of this agreement.*
>
> *2. The Parties may agree in writing to modify Annex 104.1 to include any amendment referred to in paragraph 1, and any other environment or conservation agreement.*

This provides qualified protection for the four MEAs specifically cited—as well as a few bilateral agreements among the countries—from application of NAFTA rules. When equally effective alternatives are reasonably available, then there is an obligation to choose the one that least interferes with trade. While not a full exclusion for MEAs, this is far stronger language than anything in the WTO.

The POPs convention, the Kyoto Protocol, and other MEAs that have emerged since the signing of NAFTA are not included in the above exclusion. While possible for consideration under Article 104 in the future, the Kyoto Protocol could only be considered if the other parties had agreed to implement it, which the U.S. has not. Even then there is no guarantee of their inclusion under Article 104.

> Environmental protection measures taken as a result of MEAs would have to meet the necessity test within WTO rules: they must be the least trade-restrictive option available to meet the environmental objective.

There is additional language in NAFTA Article 1114: Environmental Measures, but it is entirely ineffective at providing any protection for MEAs or other environmental measures since such measures are required to conform to NAFTA rules. NAFTA Article 1114 (2) only states that parties "should not" lower environmental standards in order to encourage investment. The only remedy provided is consultation between parties.

Some MEAs also contain trade language that helps to define the relationship of the agreement to trade treaties. The POPs Convention contains a short reference in its preamble:

*Recognizing that this Convention and other international agreements
in the field of trade and environment are mutually supportive...*

At best, this language does not subjugate the POPs Convention to trade treaties. But neither does it guarantee that actions taken by countries under the POPs Convention will be protected from the WTO or NAFTA.

The Kyoto Protocol contains a clause indicating that the countries will strive to implement the terms of the agreement in a manner that minimizes adverse effects on international trade.[66] While the Kyoto Protocol calls for parties to try and minimize impacts on international trade, it does not exclude measures taken to implement the protocol from the WTO or NAFTA.

Since the United States has not agreed to implement Kyoto, it means that Canada will not be able to argue that Kyoto should take precedence over trade obligations with the U.S. in the event that measures undertaken to implement Kyoto conflict with trade and investment obligations in either the WTO, NAFTA, or the FTAA, should it be successfully negotiated and implemented.

> Since the United States has not agreed to implement Kyoto, it means that Canada will not be able to argue that Kyoto should take precedence over trade obligations with the U.S.

The negotiation of MEAs is necessary to manage global environmental problems, and their provisions should take precedence over commercial trade treaties. It would be impossible to negotiate adequate protection for the environment within trade treaties, given their overriding concern with commercial values and objectives.

In summary:

- No part of the WTO (GATT, GATS, etc.) provides any special protection for international environmental agreements.
- Although the WTO Committee on Trade and Environment is charged with attempting to clarify the relationship between international trade rules and environmental protection agreements, the little progress made to date may have further strengthened the priority given to commercial interests.
- NAFTA contains a special qualified protection for four older MEAs and two bilateral environmental and conservation agreements (one is a U.S.-Canada agreement, and the other is a U.S.-Mexico agreement).

- MEAs also have language that references their relationship to the WTO and NAFTA, but there is no clear language that fully excludes trade challenges.
- If MEAs are not included in NAFTA Article 104, then measures taken to implement their obligations are more vulnerable to potential challenges by an investor claim for compensation, as well as state-to-state dispute action.

Notes

[1] NAFTA, Annex II, Schedule of Canada, Aboriginal Affairs, II-C-1. The measure listed in the reservations is the *Constitution Act 1982*, being Schedule B of the *Canada Act 1982* (UK), 1982, c.11.

[2] Canada, Schedule of Specific Commitments, GATS/SC/16, April 15, 1994, pages 5-6.

[3] *Economic Burden of Illness in Canada*, 1998, Health Canada, Ottawa, 1998.

[4] Commission on the Future of Health Care in Canada, *Building on Values: The Future of Health Care in Canada*, Final Report, November 2002, Roy J. Romanow, Q.C. Commissioner; page 161.

[5] Ibid., Table 7.1, page 161. These figures include all rural and remote communities across Canada.

[6] Ibid., page 162.

[7] Ibid., page 167.

[8] Ibid., page 167.

[9] Ibid., page 7.

[10] *The World Health Report 2002*, Annex Table 5: Selected National Health Accounts Indicators for all Member States, Estimates for 1995 to 2000; Canadian figures on pages 202-203 and 210-211 and U.S. figures on pages 208-209 and 216-217.

[11] GATS Article I.(c): "a service supplied in the exercise of governmental authority means any service which is supplied neither on a commercial basis nor in competition with one of more service suppliers."

[12] World Trade Organization, Council for Trade in Services, Health and Social Services, "Background Note by the Secretariat," S/C/W/50, September 18, 1998; page 11, *emphasis added*.

[13] GATS Article II most-favoured-nation treatment requires according all members with the equivalent level of treatment "… immediately and unconditionally" for like services and service suppliers.

[14] Mathew Sanger, Reckless Abandon: Canada, the GATS and the Future of Health Care, Canadian Centre for Policy Alternatives, Ottawa, 2001; pages 75-76.

[15] Romanow Report, Recommendation 5, page 248.

[16] GATS Article VI.4. Article VI.2 and VI.4 have general application. Article VI.1, VI.2 and VI.3 only apply where specific commitments are made.

[17] Ibid.

[18] GATS Article VI.4 (c).

[19] Jake Vallinga, "International Trade, Health Systems and Services: A Health Policy Perspective," Trade Policy Research 2001, January 21, 2000, page 154; http://www.dfait-maeci.gc.ca/eet/pdf/07-en.pdf.

[20] Ibid., page 156.

[21] NAFTA Annex II Canada, Social Services, II-C-9.

[22] Ibid., page 1.

[23] AIT Article 504.1 (a) and (b) Reciprocal Non-Discrimination. The language in NAFTA Article 1003 National Treatment and Non-Discrimination is similar.

[24] AIT Article 502. See NAFTA Article 1001 for its threshold levels. It is noteworthy that NAFTA has a built-in inflation-adjustment clause that would increase the thresholds, whereas the AIT has no inflation-adjustment factor. In effect, AIT thresholds are constantly falling unless the parties can agree otherwise.

[25] AIT Article 506. NAFTA Section B Articles 1008-1016.

[26] Under NAFTA the parties to the agreement also have access to state-to-state dispute procedures outlined under Chapter 20, and individual investors have access to the investor-state dispute process in Chapter 11. AIT disputes are restricted to bid-protest procedures in chapter 5.

[27] AIT Article 508. In particular see 508.2, where four tests are set out for resolving disputes for use of such programs, including proof that the program is applied only in exceptional circumstances (rarely), must be justified by evidence that the program works, minimize discrimination and assess impact on development of competitive Canadian companies.

[28] Limitations on the export of raw logs are excluded in both the Canada-US Free Trade Agreement (Article 1203: Miscellaneous Exceptions) and the NAFTA (Annex 301.3.1).

[29] (GATS/SC/16, 15 April 1994) (page 32)

[30] "Issues and Options for a Policy on Impact and Benefits Agreements," by Steven A. Kennett, Canadian Institute of Resource Law, May 3, 1999.

[31] NAFTA Article 1106: Performance Requirements sub article 1 page 11-3

[32] If another foreign investor feels it is being excluded from the competition for business opportunities as a result of the terms of the IBA, it is possible for that firm to make use of trade-treaty rules to challenge the preferential IBA rules.

[33] Kennett, page 11.

[34] Ibid., page 14.

[35] http://www.canadapost.ca/business/corporate/about/newsroom/pr/bib/popup_print-e.asp?prid=145.

[36] http://www.canadapost.ca/common/corporate/about/northern_services/what-e.asp.

[37] *Canada Post Corporation Act*, 5.(1)(a).

[38] Ibid., 5.(2)(b).

[39] Ibid., 14.(1) and 15.(1).

[40] http://www.canadapost.ca/personal/corporate/about/annual_report/eng/financial.html. See financial performance. Canada Post began to pay income taxes in 1994.

[41] http://money.cnn.com/MGI/snap/A2124.htm.

[42] Ibid., page 12.

[43] See Sinclair, pages 29-31, for a detailed discussion on the classification of services under the GATS as they relate to Canada Post. Postal services are pick-up, delivery and transport of letters, parcels and packages rendered by a national postal administration. Courier services are the same as postal services, but delivered by private service providers.

[44] National Farmers' Union Submission to the Canada Post Review, February 15, 1996.

[45] Arctic Council, Sustainable Development Working Group, SDWG 2002/A/3 23 April 2002, Draft 3; page 1.

[46] Ibid., page 2.

[47] Government of Yukon, Department of Environment, Contaminated Sites http://www.environmentyukon.gov.yk.ca/epa/coninfop.shtml.

[48] Statutes of the Yukon, 1991, Chapter 5, Part I, Environmental Rights, Arcticle 6.

[49] Ibid., Arcticle 8.

[50] Ibid., Arcticle 12 (1) and (2).

[51] Stockholm Convention on Persistent Organic Pollutants, Stockholm, 22 May 2001, http://www.pops.int/.

[52] GATT Arcticle XX (b) and (g).

[53] See Panel Report "United States – Restrictions on Imports of Tuna," adopted June 16, 1994, DS29/R, para 364-377.

[54] See Panel Report "United States – Restrictions on Imports of Tuna," adopted September 3, 1991, DSR/21/r-39S/I55, para 5.21.

[55] Samuel S. Epstein, M.D., *The Politics of Cancer* (Garden City, New York: Anchor Books, 1979); page 83.

[56] See Panel Report "Thailand – Restrictions on Importation of and Internal Taxes on Cigarettes," adopted on November 7, 1990, DS10/R – 37S/200.

[57] See Panel Report "United States – Standards for Reformulated and Conventional Gasoline," WT/DS2/R, adopted on January 29, 1996, para. 2.1.

[58] Steven Shrybman, *A Citizen's Guide to the World Trade Organization* (Canadian Centre for Policy Alternatives and James Lorimer Co. Ltd., 1999); page 87.

[59] Michelle Swenarchuk, "Civilizing Globalization: Trade and Environment, Thirteen Years On," March 7, 2001, Report No 399 ISBN 1-894158-76-8, Canadian Environmental Law Association, Toronto; page 4.

[60] See the WTO Agreement on Technical Barriers to Trade Articles 2.4-2.5 and the WTO Agreement on the Application of Sanitary and Phytosanitary Measures.

[61] See the WTO Agreement on the Application of Sanitary and Phytosanitary Measures, Arcticle 5.7

[62] NAFTA Chapter 11 Investor-State Disputes (to March 2003), Compiled by the Trade and Investment Research Project, Canadian Centre for Policy Alternatives.

[63] North American Agreement on Environmental Cooperation, between The Government of Canada, The Government of the United States and the Government of the United States of Mexico (Secretariat of the Commission for Environmental Cooperation, 1993), http://www.cec.org/site_map/index.cfm?varlan+english.

[64] "The Results of The Uruguay Round of Multilateral Trade Negotiations; The Legal Texts", GATT Secretariat Geneva, 1994, page 6

[65] "An Environmental Guide to the World Trade Organization" by Steven Shrybman, Sierra Club of Canada, May 1997; http://www.sierraclub.ca/national/trade-env/env-guide-wto.html.

[66] Kyoto Protocol to the United Nations Framework Convention on Climate Change, Article 2, paragraph 3.

PART SEVEN

Key Findings and Conclusions

GOVERNANCE

FINDING 1: Northern governments, including Aboriginal and territorial governments, do not have the same level of protection afforded to the provinces under NAFTA's Annex I reservations for investments and services or under exceptions provided for in WTO agreements for goods and services. Aboriginal governments have some additional protection provided by Annex II reservations.

CONCLUSION: The Government of Nunavut, and powers newly devolved to territorial and Aboriginal governments after the the WTO was created and NAFTA came into effect, are particularly subject to the risk of a trade challenge. This risk could be reduced if the federal government negotiated to apply the safeguards that are already available to the provinces to territorial and Aboriginal governments and to responsibilities newly devolved from the federal government. Of particular importance is the partial protection afforded the provinces under NAFTA Annex I reservations for mandating local economic spin-offs for major resource projects.

ECONOMIC DEVELOPMENT

FINDING 2: Local economic-development initiatives, including those that give preferential treatment to businesses, goods, services, or investment from territorial and Aboriginal communities, are at odds with several rules in NAFTA and the WTO and are at risk if a party to one of these trade and investment treaties, or an investor under NAFTA, challenges them.

CONCLUSION: Canada's position in WTO and FTAA negotiations should include negotiating stronger safeguards for regional economic development policies than are currently provided for in NAFTA and the WTO agreements.

FINDING 3: Altering the definition of a Canadian diamond to encourage value-added activities in the North could be inconsistent with Canada's GATS commitments, which include full coverage of services related to mining. Multinational mining companies that currently process Canadian diamonds offshore may also invoke the NAFTA investment provisions to challenge any such measures that impair their Canadian investments.

CONCLUSION: Efforts by federal and territorial governments to promote value added activities in the North should be encouraged. A trade challenge to such initiatives is possible, but would be politically sensitive and would highlight the restrictions created by Canada's trade commitments. A minimal approach to reducing the risk of a trade challenge would be to enter limitations to Canada's GATS commitments to clarify that they do not apply to measures to promote diamond cutting, polishing, and other value-added activities in the North. Efforts should also be made to limit or eliminate the application of investor-state provisions under NAFTA Chapter 11.

FINDING 4: Impact benefit agreements (IBAs) contain requirements for local economic spin-offs that are likely to be inconsistent with WTO and NAFTA rules. Nunavut land-claim agreement procedures involving the federal minister in a decisive decision-making role could mean that these agreements would be required to provide foreign investors with the best available treatment in Canada (national treatment test at the federal level), increasing the likelihood of a violation of the national-treatment rule.

CONCLUSION: Trade-treaty rules weaken the bargaining position of northern governments in negotiations with foreign investors for economic spin-offs in exchange for access to valuable natural resources. Federal involvement in the IBA process needs to be examined more carefully in order to minimize potential trade challenges.

FINDING 5: Unlike the Yukon, which gained operating authority over most resources this year, the NWT and Nunavut lack jurisdiction over minerals. This could subject IBAs for mining to the best-treatment-available-in-Canada test, increasing the risk of a national-treatment violation if challenged.

CONCLUSION: While not eliminating the threat of a successful trade challenge, the two territories would be less vulnerable to such a challenge if they had jurisdiction over sub-surface minerals.

FINDING 6: First Nations without land-claim and/or self-government treaties are also more likely to be subject to a trade test based on the best treatment available in Canada. First Nations do have some additional protections afforded under NAFTA Annex II reservations, but no protections for Annex I reservations.

CONCLUSION: First Nations would be less vulnerable to successful trade challenges with land-claim and self-government treaties firmly in place.

POSTAL SERVICES

FINDING 7: Canada's postal services, especially its courier services, are currently being challenged under NAFTA by UPS with the objective of privatizing these and related services.

CONCLUSION: The North is more dependent on a non-commercial postal service than major urban centres in the south and is more vulnerable to the negative impacts of a successful trade challenge, which could lead to higher delivery rates, poorer quality services, and/or a reduction in services.

HEALTH CARE

FINDING 8: The health status of northerners is poorer than in the provinces, and even worse for Aboriginal people. At the same time, there are fewer available health services and service providers in the North, and the overall costs of health care on a per-capita basis are twice as high as in the provinces. Telehealth service delivery (the delivery of health services through electronic means such as telephone, Internet, videoconferencing, etc.) could help to reduce costs and increase available health-care services for northerners in the future.

CONCLUSION: The Romanow Commission concluded that the public delivery of primary health services through a universal health-insurance scheme continues to be the most cost-effective approach and one that will maintain higher quality of care than the for-profit approach. Public control over telehealth is, therefore, an important goal for northern governments.

FINDING 9: Health services are vulnerable to trade challenges, especially under the WTO services rules and NAFTA's investment provisions. Exceptions and reservations for health care within these treaties are weak and do not provide complete protection as a full exclusion would. The full application of GATS and NAFTA investment rules are likely to lead to unwanted privatization in the health-care system and loss of public control.

CONCLUSION: The application of rules in trade and investment treaties to health care could lead to more privatization of services and less public control. The Romanow Commission noted that this likely would lead to an increase in health-care costs and a reduction in access to services and a decline in overall quality. Northerners, especially Aboriginal people, are more vulnerable to these impacts than other Canadians. Efforts need to be made to fully exclude health services from trade agreements, especially telehealth services.

FINDING 10: Canada has already committed our national health-insurance scheme to specific GATS rules by failing to fully exclude it from its schedule of specific commitments.

CONCLUSION: Northern governments may wish to lobby the federal government to seek exclusion for health insurance from its present GATS commitments during this round of negotiations.

FINDING 11: FTAA and GATS negotiations are promising to expand the number and strength of market-liberalizing rules that could apply to health care, as well as pressure governments to include health services under all rules. Telehealth is one potential area that could be adversely affected by negotiations for special electronic commerce rules.

CONCLUSION: Increasing the number and strength of rules applicable to health care could increase unwanted privatization and loss of public control of the health care system, especially in the North. Telehealth could fall under special rules developed for electronic commerce, which would prevent a publicly-controlled approach to electronic health-services delivery. This would harm efforts in the North to improve access to affordable and good quality health services.

THE ENVIRONMENT

FINDING 12: The North's environment is highly fragile, due in part to its harsh climate. There are two sources of environmental damage; one is a result of local development, the other a result of international issues such as global warming and the accumulation of persistent organic pollutants (POPs).

CONCLUSION: The Canadian North and the Arctic in general will be more adversely affected than most other regions in the world by the melting of the Arctic ice and greater accumulation over time of persistent organic pollutants such as DDT and PCBs. Aboriginal people and their lifestyles are more adversely affected by these threats to the environment than non-Aboriginal people. POPs accumulate in the caribou and water mammals used for subsistence diets, potentially harming their health. Global warming affects the availability of wildlife used for subsistence diets.

FINDING 13: Environmental measures are treated as being inconsistent with trade-and-investment-treaty rules unless they can be considered as exceptions. Trade panels have said that these exceptions for health and the environment must be narrowly interpreted, giving precedence to market access and other commercial values over protection of the environment. There have been no trade-dispute-panel rulings where environmental exceptions were successful as a defence. There have been several successful challenges of environmental measures under both the WTO and under NAFTA's investment provisions. As a result, Canada has paid $25 million in compensation to foreign investors and has had to rescind environmental protection measures.

CONCLUSION: If a northern environmental-protection measure is successfully challenged under NAFTA's investor-state dispute process, there could be two consequences: firstly, the environmental-protection measure may have to be weakened or entirely withdrawn; secondly, compensation claims could be large enough to have a major impact on territorial or

Aboriginal governments' finances. Territorial and Aboriginal governments may wish to know if the federal government intends to pass the costs of successful claims against sub-national measures onto the sub-national jurisdiction involved.

FINDING 14: There are several multilateral environmental agreements (MEAs) that have been signed over the years designed to deal with international environmental issues such as POPs, global warming, ozone depletion, movement of hazardous waste, and international trade in endangered species (CITES). The Stockholm Convention on POPs and the Kyoto Protocol on climate change will have a positive impact on the environment and health of the North and its people over time.

CONCLUSION: Northern governments, through such organizations as the Arctic Council, have made a difference in the successful pursuit of MEAs that protect the environment.

FINDING 15: Some MEAs have qualified protection from some trade agreements (for example, CITES in NAFTA). But there is much uncertainty about how trade and investment treaties would affect the enforcement of MEAs. Strong arguments can be made that MEAs are international environmental standards that could be deemed to be consistent with trade-and-investment-treaty rules. Problems, however, could arise if two nations are parties to a trade agreement but are not party to the same MEAs. NAFTA's investor-state dispute process and investment rules pose a threat to MEAs, even when both NAFTA countries are parties to an MEA in dispute. State-to-state disputes involving other NAFTA chapters are also possible threats.

CONCLUSION: MEAs are more likely than domestic environmental-protection measures to withstand trade-and-investment-treaty challenges. However, great uncertainty remains about the status of the relationship between MEAs and trade and investment treaties. Given a greater vested interest in MEAs' success, northern governments may want to have the federal government ensure that MEAs' exposure to trade and investment treat challenges are minimized, if not eliminated.

FINDING 16: There are continuous efforts to broaden and deepen trade-and-investment-treaty rules through negotiations. New GATS and FTAA negotiations are now taking place. If successful in their efforts to expand coverage and to increase the numbers and strength of rules, these new trade and investment treaties will increase the risk of successful trade challenges against measures by northern governments. Economic-development initiatives, infrastructure services, social services, and environmental-protection measures will face even greater risks in the future posed by challenges under trade and investment treaties.

CONCLUSION: The new rules will increase the risks posed by trade-and-investment-treaty challenges and will undermine the new governments and authorities recently won by people of the North. There is a fundamental and underlying conflict between the commercial objectives of these treaties and the needs of northern peoples to have services provided that are affordable and meet their special needs. Northern governments may wish to inform the federal government of their concerns and special needs, as well as ensure that they are obtaining full transparency on sensitive negotiations.

ACRONYMS

AIT	Agreement on Internal Trade
FTAA	Free Trade Agreement of the Americas
GATT	General Agreement on Tariffs and Trade (sometimes used to describe the world trade regime that existed before the WTO began in 1994)
GATS	General Agreement on Trade in Services
IBAs	Impact Benefit Agreements
ISO	International Standards Organization
MEAs	Multilateral Environmental Agreements
NAFTA	North American Free Trade Agreement
POPs	Stockholm Convention on Persistent Organic Pollutants
TRIMS	Agreement on Trade Related Investment Measures
TRIPS	Agreement on Trade Related Intellectual Property Rights
WTO	World Trade Organization